Elite • 251

The US Marine Corps 1775–1859

Continental and United States Marines

RON FIELD

ILLUSTRATED BY ADAM HOOK

Series editors Martin Windrow & Nick Reynolds

OSPREY PUBLISHING
Bloomsbury Publishing Plc
Kemp House, Chawley Park, Cumnor Hill, Oxford OX2 9PH, UK
29 Earlsfort Terrace, Dublin 2, Ireland
1385 Broadway, 5th Floor, New York, NY 10018, USA
E-mail: info@ospreypublishing.com
www.ospreypublishing.com

OSPREY is a trademark of Osprey Publishing Ltd

First published in Great Britain in 2023

© Osprey Publishing Ltd, 2023

A catalog record for this book is available from the British Library.

ISBN: PB 9781472851543; eBook 9781472851550;
ePDF 9781472851536; XML 9781472851529

23 24 25 26 27   10 9 8 7 6 5 4 3 2 1

Index by Rob Munro
Typeset by PDQ Digital Media Solutions, Bungay, UK
Printed and bound in India by Replika Press Private Ltd.

Osprey Publishing supports the Woodland Trust, the UK's leading woodland conservation charity.

To find out more about our authors and books visit
www.ospreypublishing.com. Here you will find extracts, author interviews, details of forthcoming events and the option to sign up for our newsletter.

Acknowledgments

Joan Thomas, Art Curator, Owen Linlithgow Conner, Curator, Uniforms and Heraldry, and Jonathan Bernstein, Curator of Arms and Armor, National Museum of the Marine Corps, Quantico, VA; Gale Munro, Head Curator, Navy Art Collection, Naval History & Heritage Command, Washington Navy Yard, DC; Peter Harrington, Curator at the Anne S.K. Brown Military Collection, RI; Stephen Wise; Fred Gaede; Don Troiani; Bruce B. Herman; Ron Coddington; Dr. William Schultz; and Lieutenant Colonel Charles C. Cureton, USMCR (Ret.), for generously sharing his extensive knowledge of the uniforms and equipage of the United States Marine Corps.

Artist's note

Readers may care to note that the original paintings from which the color plates in this book were prepared are available for private sale. All reproduction copyright whatsoever is retained by the publishers. All inquiries should be addressed to:

scorpiopaintings@btinternet.com

The publishers regret that they can enter into no correspondence upon this matter.

Front cover, above: "The Assault on Derna," painted by Colonel Charles H. Waterhouse, USMCR (Ret.), depicts the moment First Lieutenant Presley N. O'Bannon and his squad of Marines helped capture the Tripolitan fortress at Derna on April 27, 1805. (Art Collection, National Museum of the Marine Corps: Accession Number: 29-454)

Title-page illustration: Lieutenant Josiah Watson posed for this sixth-plate daguerreotype portrait about 1846, clothed in the undress lieutenant's uniform following the 1839 Regulations. Prominently displayed is his cap, which features a foul anchor in the center of a wreath. Watson was commissioned a second lieutenant in 1835 and served in Florida during the Second Seminole War, being stationed at Fort Brooke in 1836. Promoted to first lieutenant, he formed part of the First Marine Battalion in Mexico in 1847. Achieving the rank of major, he died of tuberculosis on February 5, 1864. (Collection of Dr. William Schultz)

CONTENTS

THE US MARINE CORPS 1775–1859

CONTINENTAL AND UNITED STATES MARINES

THE AMERICAN REVOLUTIONARY WAR

The first American Marines were organized on November 10, 1775, when the Second Continental Congress (1775–81) passed a resolution sponsored by Massachusetts delegate John Adams to raise "two Battalions of marines … consisting of one Colonel, two Lieutenant Colonels, two Majors, and other officers …" Prior to this, seven of the original 13 American colonies had organized their own Marine forces to serve aboard the ships of their embryonic navies. On November 28, 1775, Samuel Nicholas, a blacksmith's son from Pennsylvania, was commissioned the first officer of the Continental Marines, and on December 3, the American ship-of-war *Alfred* went into commission with Captain Nicholas commanding her Marine detachment. Nicholas remained the senior Marine officer throughout the American Revolutionary War (1775–83) and is considered to be the first Marine Commandant. The recruits who gathered at the Tun Tavern, a hostelry on the east side of King Street, Philadelphia, in November 1775 were required to be "good seamen, or so acquainted with maritime affairs," and that they be enlisted "to serve for and during the present war between Great Britain and the colonies" (*Journal of the Continental Congress*, Vol. 3: 348).

Major Samuel Nicholas, first Commandant of the Continental Marines, wears an example of the green coat faced with white first prescribed for the Marines on September 5, 1776. Based on a photograph of a now-missing 18th-century miniature, this painting is by Colonel Donna J. Neary, USMCR. (Art Collection, National Museum of the Marine Corps. Accession Number: 119-2-40)

The Continental Marines distinguished themselves in a number of important operations on land and at sea during the American Revolutionary War. On February 17, 1776, a squadron of five Continental Navy vessels commanded by Commodore Esek Hopkins sailed from Cape Henlopen, Delaware, to launch an amphibious assault on New Providence Island in the British Bahamas. Arriving off Abaco, one of the islands north of New Providence Island, on March 1, Hopkins' squadron captured two sloops and he determined to attack the forts on the main island.

On March 3, 1776, Nicholas led 268 green-coated Marines and blue-jacketed sailors ashore from the two captured sloops, the schooner *Wasp*, and the sloop-of-war *Providence*, in a raid to secure much-needed supplies of munitions and gunpowder for the Continental Army. The Marines remained below deck until the vessels had anchored in the harbor close enough to reach the shore in small boats. By 0300hrs, they had captured Fort Montagu, at the eastern end of the island. Lieutenant John Trevett recalled that he took command of one of the companies and marched to the first fort. The British fired a few 18-pound shots, which did no damage. A British

officer then approached Trevett with a flag of truce, and asked what his business was, but surrendered after further shelling following which Trevett and his Marines spent the night in the fort (Clark 1969: 4.153). Although he had received a warning that the Americans might attack, Governor Montfort Browne had been caught off guard when the Continental Navy ships arrived off New Providence Island, and rushed to Government House in his nightshirt to order the firing of signal cannon to summon the militia.

The next morning the Marines marched into Nassau, the island capital, by which time Browne had ordered the transfer of most of the island's gunpowder stores onboard the schooner HMS *St. John*, commanded by Lieutenant John Grant, which set sail for St. Augustine, the capital of British East Florida. As a result, the Marines managed to capture only 20 casks of gunpowder plus 88 guns, 15 mortars, and a large quantity of shells and round shot. With 12 other high-ranking hostages, Browne was transported to New London, Connecticut, by the American squadron where he was paroled and exchanged (Clark 1969: 4.171).

Nearing the end of its homeward voyage, Hopkins' squadron encountered and exchanged shots with the British 24-gun frigate HMS *Glasgow* off the coast of Long Island, New York, on April 6, 1776. During the engagement, seven Marines were killed, and ten wounded. Commanding the Marines on the quarter deck of the *Alfred*, Second Lieutenant John Fitzpatrick fell dead after a musket ball struck him in the head. Nicholas wrote later that he had lost a worthy officer, sincere friend and companion, who was respected by the whole ship's company (Clark 1969: 4.751). Aboard the brigantine *Cabot*, Hopkins' flagship, Second Lieutenant James H. Wilson was seriously wounded and later died. Privates Patrick Kaine and George Kennedy were killed (Field 1898: 121). The Marines had been blooded. Arriving

This oil painting on canvas by V. Zveg (a pseudonym for Vladimir V. Zveguintsov) depicts green-coated Continental Marines and blue-jacketed sailors landing on New Providence Island in the Bahamas on March 3, 1776. Their initial objective, Fort Montagu, stands in the left distance. Close offshore are the vessels used to transport the landing force close into the beach. From left to right they are the two captured sloops, the schooner *Wasp*, and the sloop-of-war *Providence*. The other ships of the Continental Navy squadron are in the distance. (US Naval History and Heritage Command NH 79419-KN)

Entitled "A Marine Lieutenant dies," this painting by Colonel Charles H. Waterhouse, USMCR (Ret.), depicts the death of Second Lieutenant John Fitzpatrick, who was killed by a musket ball to the head while commanding the Marines aboard the ship-of-war *Alfred* during the action with the 24-gun frigate HMS *Glasgow* off the coast of Long Island, New York, on April 6, 1776. (Art Collection, National Museum of the Marine Corps: Accession Number: 29-4-336)

at Newport, Rhode Island, Nicholas received the congratulations of John Hancock, President of the Continental Congress, and George Washington paid his respects to the whole fleet.

Rewarded with a major's commission on June 25, 1776, Nicholas continued to recruit four more companies of Marines for the Continental Navy frigates then being built in Philadelphia. As the Board of Admiralty stipulated that a major of Marines should serve at sea on a ship-of-the-line, which the United States at that time did not possess, Nicholas was forced to remain land bound, often behind a desk, for the remainder of the war. Nevertheless, he participated in several important battles alongside the Continental Army.

Since August 1776, British forces under General William Howe had been forcing the Continental Army south out of New York. On November 16 the British overran Fort Washington in Manhattan, taking 2,837 Americans prisoner. In December Nicholas was ordered to join George Washington's army with a three-company battalion of Marines under Captains Robert Mullen (alias Mullan), Benjamin Dean, and Andrew Porter. This battalion took part in crossing the frozen Delaware River and a successful assault on the Hessians, or German auxiliaries, of the British Army, at the first battle of Trenton on December 26. On January 2, 1777, these Marines played a vital role in the withdrawal from Assunpink Creek during the second battle of Trenton. The next day Nicholas's Marines participated in Washington's decisive victory at Princeton as part of Colonel John Cadwalader's brigade, following which they shared the icy fortunes of the Continental Army in winter camp at Morristown, New Jersey. After this they reported back to Philadelphia for further duty during February 1777.

Onboard ship, Continental Marine detachments served much farther afield. Two raids on British soil involving Marines from the sloop-of-war *Ranger*, commanded by Captain John Paul Jones, are among only a handful of successful hostile landings on British soil since 1066. One of the most daring and successful naval commanders of the American Revolutionary War, Scottish-born Jones was commissioned a first lieutenant on December 7, 1775, and served on the first Continental Navy flagship, *Alfred*. Quickly promoted to captain in 1776, he was given command of the *Providence*, which destroyed British fisheries in Nova Scotia and captured 16 prize British ships.

Jones's first raids on England aboard the *Ranger* took place at Whitehaven, at the mouth of the Solway Firth, beginning on the night of April 22, 1778. He planned to seize a fort and lunette battery that defended the port, and then set fire to numerous vessels stranded in low water by the ebb tide. With Jones personally leading the expedition of 30 volunteers armed with pistols and cutlasses, among whom was First Lieutenant Samuel Wallingford of the Continental Marines, the raiding party set out at 2300hrs in two small boats from the *Ranger*, which stood 2 miles off the coast, and rowed toward the harbor. After rowing against the tide for about three hours, the expedition tried to make a landing on the coast near Saltom Pit, south of Whitehaven, in order to advance along the shore and attack the guns of the lunette battery, but the sea was rough and the shore too rocky to land. Having lost about a half-hour of darkness, the expedition next rowed past the battery and around the New Quay into the harbor as first light appeared over the hills behind Whitehaven on the morning of April 23. Landing on the

Depicted in this miniature produced in Paris, France, by an unknown artist, is Captain Matthew Parke of the Continental Marines, who served in European waters aboard the sloop-of-war *Ranger* and the frigate *Alliance* during 1777–80. He wears a green coat with white facings; a white vest, with silver buttons as prescribed for officers in 1776; and one small silver epaulet on his right shoulder, commensurate with his rank as captain. (US Navy Art Collection Acc. No: 72-189-B)

quayside, Wallingford's detachment was directed to set fire to the shipping on the north side of the harbor, while Jones concentrated on the same action on the south side after taking the fort and spiking the guns. Both parties had lighted candles and combustible torches with which to set the vessels afire. Although the guns were successfully spiked, setting fire to the vessels proved more difficult as the candles went out failing to ignite larger fires. Only after acquiring a light by forcing entry into a nearby cottage were they able to kindle a fire in the coal ship *Thompson*. The fire failed to spread to smaller vessels alongside, however, and was eventually extinguished by fire engines brought to the quayside after the alarm had been raised by a deserter from Jones' raiding party. With flames leaping into the air from a single burning ship, the Americans returned to *Ranger* (CM, Apr. 27, 1778: 3.2).

Later the same day Jones landed a raiding party on St. Mary's Isle, a narrow peninsula jutting out at the north end of the Solway Firth, hoping to take the Earl of Selkirk as a hostage to be traded for American sailors impressed in the Royal Navy. With the Earl absent in London, the raiders contented themselves with carrying off the family silver. The Countess of Selkirk later recalled the "vile blackguard look" of one of the American naval officers present, but remarked on the good behavior of "a civil young man in a green uniform, an anchor on his buttons ... [who] seemed naturally well bred" (quoted in de Koven 1913: 1.310). During this operation, Wallingford was the only American killed, when *Ranger* exchanged shots with the sloop-of-war HMS *Drake* 24 hours later. Five of the British crew were killed, including the captain, and the vessel surrendered to Jones. Jones subsequently wrote to the Countess from France promising the return of her silver, which was done seven years later.

Jones continued to operate off the British Isles and by the summer of 1779 commanded the 42-gun ship-of-war *Bonhomme Richard*, a merchant ship rebuilt and given to America by the French shipping magnate, Jacques-

Donatien Le Ray de Chaumont. The Marines serving aboard this vessel consisted of a detachment of the Infanterie Irlandaise, Régiment de Walsh-Serrant, on loan from King Louis XVI of France. Dressed in scarlet coats with blue facings, and commanded by Irish officers, these men played a vital role as sharpshooters, losing 67 killed, during Jones' victory over the fifth rate HMS *Serapis* at the battle of Flamborough Head off the east coast of England on September 23, 1779.

Marines under Captain John Welsh were involved in an abortive attempt to capture a British fort at Penobscot Bay in Maine on July 24, 1779. A force of 1,200 men, including 300 Marines, conducted an amphibious assault and scaled a 200ft-high cliff, driving off the defenders, who consisted of 450 men of the 74th Regiment of (Highland) Foot, and 200 men of the 82nd (Duke of Hamilton's) Regiment of Foot. The failure of the Continental Navy commander to provide further support, and the arrival of a Royal Navy squadron that drove off the American vessels, left the Marines plus some sailors and militia stranded on the coast. Retiring southward, most of the sea soldiers found their way back through about 270 miles of wilderness to the nearest American settlements along the Kennebec River.

The Treaty of Paris of September 3, 1783, brought an end to the American Revolutionary War and ensured the independence of the 13 original states. As the last of the Continental Navy's ships were sold, the Navy and Marines were disbanded. During the next ten years, the young American nation was largely defenseless against foreign aggression as the Royal Navy, French privateers, and Algerian corsairs wreaked havoc among its merchant shipping.

Uniform, arms, and equipment 1775–83

For the first few months of their service, the Continental Marines appear to have improvised with regard to uniforms, and Captain Nicholas outfitted his original enlistees from whatever sources he could find. Finally, on September 5, 1776, the Continental Marine Committee of Congress prescribed the uniform for Marine officers as "A Green Coat faced with white, Round Cuffs, Slash'd Sleeves and Pockets; with Buttons round the Cuff, Silver epaulette on the right Shoulder – Skirts turn'd back, Buttons to suit the Faceings. White waistcoat [vest] and Brieches edged with Green, Black Gaiters and Garters ..." (Sherburne 1825: 28). Buttons were silver and carried a foul anchor.

A

CONTINENTAL MARINES, 1775

A captain, private, and musician of the Continental Marines stand in front of the Tun Tavern on King Street, Philadelphia, which served as their recruiting depot in 1775. The hair of all three men is queued and whitened with flour.

Wearing a *chapeau* with black silk cockade, the officer (**1**) has a small silver epaulet on the right shoulder of his green coat with white facings. His green-edged white vest has flapped pockets on the skirts. His fall-front breeches are secured at each knee with buttons and a small buckle. Held in place with garters, his white silk stockings and straight-last shoes are protected by black canvas half-gaiters. He is armed with an Army-pattern sword with gilt hilt and black leather scabbard, carried in a frog attached to a black leather shoulder belt.

The headgear of the private (**2**) consists of a black felt "common hat" with white trim and black silk cockade

pinning up the brim. Although basically of the same pattern as that worn by officers, his coat with scarlet facings is of coarser cloth, as is his untrimmed vest. His breeches are of imperfectly bleached cloth and his off-white coarse wool stockings are without gaiters. A black leather stock around his neck aids a correct military posture. He carries at shoulder arms a .69-caliber Model 1766 Charleville Marine flintlock musket. A brush and pricker set for cleaning the touch hole and lock of his musket hangs from a whitened buff leather shoulder belt.

Wearing the same pattern of uniform, the youthful musician (**3**) beats a drum suspended from a whitened buff leather sling, and painted with a "coiled rattlesnake" beneath which is the motto "Don't Tread on Me!" This motto was first observed by a citizen of Philadelphia while the Marines were being recruited in December 1775.

Given less consideration by the Continental Marine Committee, enlisted Marines were to wear green shirts "if they can be procured," as a stopgap until proper uniforms could be obtained (Sherburne 1825: 28). Some enlisted men may have received full uniforms at this time. On November 13, 1776, a Philadelphia newspaper published a reward for the capture of a runaway servant of German origin who stole clothing from his master resident in Darby, Chester County, Pennsylvania, which included "one green regimental coat lined and faced with white, with large metal buttons" (*PG & WA*, Nov. 13, 1776: 2.3).

Following the Treaty of Alliance of February 6, 1778, Congress purchased uniforms for the Marines from France. The Marine detachment aboard the frigate *Boston*, which carried John Adams, the newly appointed commissioner to France, across the Atlantic, were on arrival at Bordeaux issued with French-made uniforms. On May 13, Second Lieutenant William Jennison, Jr., entered in his private journal: "Regimentals for the Marines and ordered by Congress were brought aboard and distributed to all officers and men"; they consisted of "40 Green coats faced with White, 40 White Waistcoats, 40 White Breeches, The Buttons for the whole to be plain white. Coats to be open sleeved and a Belt to every Waistcoat" (Collum 1891: 104). Made of pewter rather than white metal, buttons for enlisted Marines bore a foul anchor.

On July 15, 1779, Secretary of the Continental Marine Committee Joseph Pennell drafted a list of more clothing to be imported for the Marines, which was submitted by Benjamin Franklin, Commissioner of the Continental Congress at the Court of Versailles, to the French Minister of Foreign Affairs, the Comte de Vergennes, on September 10 of that year. The list consisted of:

> 1000 yds green Cloth …1000 yds white Cloth … 2000 yds of white Shalloon [or coat lining], 14 lb white hair Twist … 35 lb white thread, 32 lb green thread, 1500 Doz. White Metal or Pewter Coat Buttons, 1250 Doz. White Metal or Pewter Vest Buttons, 50 Pieces of Russia Sheeting [possibly for knapsacks], 5000 yards of Oznabrigs [Osnaburg], 1000 yds of Russia Drab [possibly for waistcoats and breeches], 1000 yds best white Flannel [for shirts], 1800 yds of Dowlas [coarse cloth possibly for lining or gaiters]. (Transcript, LOC)

The detachments of Continental Marines serving in European waters under Captain John Paul Jones were differently clad. Although First Lieutenant Samuel Wallingford, commanding the Marine detachment aboard Jones's *Ranger*, wore the regulation green, the Marines aboard the *Bonhomme Richard*, another vessel Jones commanded, were dressed otherwise according to John Adams. In his diary on May 13, 1779, Adams wrote:

> After dinner, walked out with Captain Jones … to see Jones's Marines, dressed in the English uniform, scarlet and white. A number of very active and clever sergeants and corporals are employed to teach them the exercises, and manoeuvres & marches … after which, Jones came on board our ship [the frigate *Alliance*] … You see the character of the man in his uniform, and that of his officers and Marines, variant from the uniforms established by Congress – golden button-holes for himself, two epaulettes, marines in red and white, instead of green. (Adams 1851: 152)

The Marines under Jones' command consisted of a detachment of 137 men of the Infanterie Irlandaise, Régiment de Walsh-Serrant. Known as the "Wild

John Adams, appointed the United States' commissioner to France in 1779, reviews the red-coated Infanterie Irlandaise, Régiment de Walsh-Serrant, a unit that served as Marines on board *Bonhomme Richard*, commanded by Captain John Paul Jones. (Art Collection, National Museum of the Marine Corps: Accession No. 2012.1026.332)

Geese," they were Jacobite exiles from Ireland, some recent and others the descendants of men who had migrated to France over the last 100 years, and served in the French Army. Commanded by Irish officers, they wore scarlet coats, albeit with blue facings, to remind the English that Jacobites, as supporters of the legitimate Stuart monarchy of England, had more right to wear those colors than did the supporters of George the Elector of Hanover. They were to play a vital role as sharpshooters during Jones's victory over HMS *Serapis* at the battle of Flamborough Head off the east coast of England on September 23, 1779.

For reasons unknown, the facing color of the green-coated Continental Marine uniform was changed from white to scarlet in 1779. A description of deserters from Captain Robert Mullan's company published in the *Pennsylvania Gazette* on November 10 of that year stated that both Privates William Warner and John MacKeanay ran off in their regimentals consisting of "a green coat with red facings, white woollen jacket [or vest with sleeves], a pair of light coloured cloth breeches, woollen ſtockings, a round hat, with white binding, and new ſhoes" (*PG & WA*, Nov. 10, 1779: 3.3).

The Continental Marines were initially issued with whatever arms were available. Whether captured or acquired, these would probably have been the British .75-caliber Long Land Pattern "Brown Bess" flintlock musket. Also issued was the British .75-caliber Sea Service Pattern musket. About 38in in length, this weapon was much handier for maneuvering about in cramped quarters aboard ship. It also had brass fittings that were less susceptible to corrosion at sea. Many of these weapons were replaced with the .69-caliber Model 1766 Charleville Marine flintlock musket, also with brass fittings, which the Continental Congress purchased from France. Also carried was a small sword that hung from the waist belt. Cartridges were carried in a Pattern 1775–83 black leather cartridge box, which carried 24 rounds and was suspended over the left shoulder from a plain whitened buff bridle leather or linen webbing sling. A brush and pricker set for cleaning the touch hole and lock of the musket was carried by each man, suspended from the cartridge-box sling.

THE BIRTH OF THE US MARINE CORPS

In 1794 the US Congress reactivated the Navy with the passage of an Act providing for the construction of six frigates, and the recruitment of an adequate number of seamen and Marines to man them. Thus the authorized strength of the United States Marine Corps was established at six lieutenants, six sergeants, 12 corporals, six drummers, six fifers, and 280 privates, or a total of 316 officers and men (McClellan 1925: 1.9.3). Some of the earliest recruits were infantrymen from the Legion of the United States. Those volunteering for sea service as Marines aboard the frigate USS *Constellation* were advised by Lieutenant Samuel T. Dyson, 1st Artillerists & Engineers, on May 30, 1798, that they would be returned to the Legion on completion of their cruise (PWD 1798: zxx07).

During the period of construction of the vessels, Marines were used to guard them. The exact date of the first commission given a Marine officer or the date of the first Marine enlisted is not known. That there were Marines aboard the frigate USS *United States* as early as August 17, 1797, however, is indicated by a letter from Secretary of War James McHenry to John Harris, Military Store Keeper at Philadelphia, requesting they be uniformed (PWD 1797: zzk07a). It was not until July 11, 1798, that the United States Marine Corps was formally established, to consist of one major, four captains, 16 first lieutenants, 12 second lieutenants, 48 sergeants, 48 corporals, 32 drums and fifes, and 720 privates, with William W. Burrows, of Charleston, South Carolina, appointed as Major Commandant. Additional ranks established for shore duty consisted of an adjutant, paymaster, quartermaster, sergeant-major, quartermaster-sergeant, and drum and fife-major (*Debates* 1798: 594–96). Originally based in Philadelphia, Marine Headquarters was relocated to a site near the Navy Yard in the new federal capital at Washington during June 1800.

The earliest action seen by the fledgling Marine Corps was against the French Navy. Relations with France had deteriorated in 1794 as a result of the US refusal to repay the remaining debt to Revolutionary France on the grounds that it had been owed to the previous Royalist regime for military support during the American Revolutionary War. As a result, French privateers had been seizing American merchant shipping and impressing their seamen.

Finally in 1798 President John Adams acknowledged that his country was engaged in an undeclared quasi-naval war with France, which led to several significant single-ship actions. The most important of these took place off the Island of Nevis in the West Indies on February 9, 1799, and involved *Constellation*, commanded by Commodore Thomas Truxtun, and the French frigate *L'Insurgente*, commanded by Capitaine de Frégate Michel-Pierre Barreaut. The 42-man Marine detachment aboard *Constellation*, under First Lieutenant Bartholomew Clinch, was formed in close order on the quarterdeck as the two vessels converged. Once the action had commenced, fire from the Marines had a terrible effect on the Frenchmen as the Marines aimed at gun ports, tops, and rigging, or wherever an enemy might be visible, while fire from the American frigate's great guns wreaked havoc on the French frigate. Finally, after 74 minutes of action, of which about an hour was at close quarters, *L'Insurgente* struck its colors, having sustained massive damage. The Marines suffered no casualties, while one American sailor was killed and two were wounded (McClellan 1925: 1.1213). The French sustained 40 killed and "a great many wounded" (*SCSG*, Feb. 26, 1799: 3.2).

The day after the battle Truxtun thanked the officers, sailors, and Marines for their bravery. In a letter to Burrows he highly commended Clinch's actions, and presented the second-best sword captured from the French to the young Marine officer (McClellan 1925: 1.12.14).

The new Marine Corps conducted its first landing on a foreign shore on May 11, 1800, when 90 men of the frigate USS *Constitution*, including a detachment of Marines commanded by Captain Daniel Carmick, took part in a raid on French shipping at Puerto Plata on the north coast of the Spanish island of Santo Domingo. Entering the harbor of Bay Chouchoux undetected at about 1000hrs with his men below decks in *Sally*, a commandeered American sloop, Carmick later recalled that the operation reminded him of the wooden horse of Troy (McClellan 1925: 1.13.6). Drawing quietly alongside the six-gun corvette *Sandwich*, a captured British vessel held in the harbor by the French, the Marines rushed onboard yelling like "devils" and took its crew completely by surprise. Carmick's command next waded ashore in water up to their necks to spike the three guns in Fortaleza San Felipe before the commanding officer had time to react or obtain reinforcement from the city. Back onboard *Sally* in about an hour from the time *Sandwich* was captured, the Marines, and sailors accompanying the expedition, made ready the sloop's guns and prepared for an attack from the shore that did not come. Sailing out at 0200hrs the next morning, *Sandwich* and *Sally* joined *Constitution* out at sea. Although acclaimed as a resounding success, the attack proved to be a breach of Spain's nominal neutrality, and the US Navy was required to return *Sandwich* to the French.

This profile engraving of Major Daniel Carmick was produced by Charles B.J. Févret de Saint-Mémin. Carmick conducted the US Marine Corps' first landing on a foreign shore on May 11, 1800. Wounded by a British Congreve rocket during the attack on New Orleans on December 23, 1814, he never fully recovered and died on November 6, 1816. At that time, he was the second-highest-ranking officer in the Marine Corps. (Library of Congress LC-DIG-pga-13198)

Uniform, arms, and equipment 1797–1804

In a letter written on August 24, 1797, to Captain John Barry, commander of the *United States*, Secretary of War James McHenry wrote:

> In order that a perfect uniformity of dreſs may be obtained by the officers, marines, and others, on board the Ships of War which may be employed in the service of the United States, I tranſmit you incloſed, the regulations which have been established for this purpose, and to which you, and all under your command will be pleased to pay some respect. (PWD 1797: 0001 xjz11)

According to the 1797 Regulations, Marine Corps officers wore a uniform dress consisting of a dark-blue coat lined with scarlet, with long scarlet lapels, standing collar, cuffs, skirts, and pocket flaps. Buttons of yellow metal bore a foul anchor and eagle, with nine on each lapel, one either side of the collar, and three on pocket flaps and slash cuffs. A scarlet vest with skirts had a single row of buttons, and two plain pocket flaps. A captain was distinguished by a small gold epaulet on the right shoulder and a gold counter-epaulet without fringe on the left shoulder. Senior lieutenants commanding a guard aboard ship wore a gold epaulet on the right shoulder, and the junior lieutenant, if there was one, wore a gold epaulet on the left shoulder. Breeches were plain dark blue, and white for warm weather. Headgear consisted of a cocked hat with black silk cockade, and officers were to carry a yellow-mounted small sword.

In a letter to First Lieutenant Reuben Lilly on October 26, 1789, Major Commandant Burrows stated that the fatigue dress for officers consisted of "a plain blue frock, lapelled, naval buttons … white vest and breeches, with same buttons" (McClellan 1925: 1.9.37, fn. 40).

As the Marine Corps and the Navy were part of the War Department at this time, enlisted Marines were issued surplus Pattern 1787 riflemen's clothing drawn from the Army quartermaster department in Philadelphia and adapted for Marine service. For example, on August 17, 1797, Military Store Keeper John Harris was ordered to deliver "Rifle Coats" for ten sergeants and 162 privates of the Marines serving on "the Frigates" (PWD 1797: zel23). Originally prescribed for the Army's Legionary Corps on January 30, 1787, these coats were dark blue with scarlet facings and shoulder wings (PWD 1797: xxa1a).

This was not too dissimilar to the coat style prescribed for the Marine Corps later that year, which consisted of a short dark-blue coatee with scarlet "turnbacks," wings, and lapels that also ran around the skirts of the garment. Nine small foul-anchor-and-eagle buttons were attached to each lapel. Three buttons of the same size and pattern were sewn around each cuff, with six buttons on the rear skirts and three on each pocket on the skirts. The vest was scarlet, and dark-blue breeches were trimmed with a scarlet welt inserted into the outside seam. White linen overalls were worn in the summer months. There was no mention of headgear for enlisted men at this stage.

The uniform of NCOs was in general the same as that worn by privates except it was made of better material. Sergeants wore two small yellow silk epaulets and corporals one. Sergeants carried brass-handled swords supplied from Army arsenals, being either French or British grenadier swords acquired during the American Revolutionary War (McClellan 1925: 1.11.20).

As formal uniform regulations for Marines were not produced until March 25, 1804, a fuller description of uniforms supplied prior to that date can only be produced from correspondence between the Commandant of the Marine Corps and his officers, as well as Navy Agent purchase records and inventories/invoices.

By late 1779, the Navy Department began ordering replacement clothing and equipment using Army patterns. The procurement of uniforms was not centralized until the mid-1820s. Hence, Navy Agents acquired clothing and equipment in each of the principal ports along the Eastern Seaboard, which

MARINES ABOARD USS *CONSTELLATION*, 1799

B In action against the French frigate *L'Insurgente* off the Island of Nevis in the West Indies on February 9, 1799, the Marines under First Lieutenant Bartholomew Clinch form on the quarterdeck of the frigate USS *Constellation* as the two vessels converge. Once the action began, their fire – aimed at gun ports, tops, and rigging – would take a terrible toll on the Frenchmen, who sustained 40 killed and many wounded. Finally, after 74 minutes of action of which about an hour was at close quarters, *L'Insurgente* struck its colors having sustained massive damage.

The first lieutenant (**1**) in *chapeau* with red feather plume, and rank distinguished by a small gold-fringed strap or epaulet on the right shoulder, waves his British Pattern 1796

infantry officer's sword as he encourages his men to keep up their fire. His scarlet-faced coat is worn over a scarlet vest, and his white cotton, fall-front pantaloons are tucked into Hessian-style boots.

With rank indicated by two yellow silk straps over red wings, a red worsted pompon on the left of his hat, and an NCO's sword, the sergeant (**2**) wears a short coatee with a "belt" of scarlet facing running from its front around to its tails. Black leather shoulder belts support his sword, bayonet, and cartridge box.

Wearing the same pattern uniform minus pompon and yellow silk shoulder straps, the private (**3**) takes aim with his 1794 contract .69-caliber "Charleville" French-pattern musket.

resulted in some variation in dress between Marine Corps units serving aboard ship or stationed at various barracks. At Baltimore, merchant and ship owner Jeremiah Yellott served as a Navy Agent and was instructed on July 26, 1798 to acquire "Plain short coats of blue, and a red belt [,] edged with red and trimed [sic] up with the same, with common small naval buttons[,] with blue pantaloons edged with red and red Vests" (McClellan 1925: 1.9.37–38, fn. 41).

In the absence of prescribed headgear, enlisted Marines initially wore surplus Army hats until October 26, 1798, when Burrows advised Lilly that they should wear a "common hat trimmed with yellow, turned up on the left side with a leather cockade" (MCA). Both the Army hat and those acquired by the Marine Corps were essentially "common hats," or full-brimmed hats worn by civilians. Largely not fit for purpose, their shape often caused problems at sea. On February 24, 1800, First Lieutenant Benjamin Strother wrote to Burrows, "Hats Continually Blown Overboard" (MCA). Earlier, on May 13, 1799, First Lieutenant David Stickney aboard the steam frigate USS *Merrimack* at Nantucket Road, off the Massachusetts coast, wrote:

A number of the Marines have lost their hats overboard by accident, and I have procured others for them … The hats that I received from the agent … were of a bad quality. After they had been wet a few times they cracked and broke very much, so badly that some are worn out, and I have replaced them by others. (MCA)

In keeping with military custom of the day, the color of Marine musicians' uniforms was reversed. On January 9, 1799, Burrows advised First Lieutenant Philip Edwards that this consisted of a "Red cloth coat with a blue belt edged with common yellow livery," plus blue collar, cuffs, shoulder straps, and wings trimmed in the same manner (MCA). Musicians' vests were also blue (PWD 1798: xlg21).

Enlisted men's hair was queued and powdered with flour when on duty, and a piece of black leather was sewn in the rear of the hat "to avoid the powder" staining it (McClellan 1925: 1.9.6). Pull-over shirts were white linen.

A European military influence brought to America during the second half of the 18th century, black leather neck stocks were worn by both Marine officers and men to provide a military bearing by keeping the man's chin up. Although later replaced by silk cravats for officers when off-duty, leather stocks were prescribed for dress until the 1870s (McClellan 1925: 1.11.6).

As enlisted Marines were often expected to perform manual tasks, as well as guard duty, aboard ship that dirtied their full-dress uniforms, some officers requested slops or sailor clothing for them. On June 13, 1799, First Lieutenant Diamond Colton at Newport, RI, advised Burrows, "I think it very necessary that they have some sort of garment for them to do their dirty work in, as their Uniform allowed by Government will not last them not more than one half the year. Ours are all to rags now" (MCA). On August 24 of the same year, Carmick wrote from Hampton Roads, "I find it impossible to keep my men clean[,] they must be granted a sailor suit of clothes besides their uniform if it is expected for them to be kept decent …" (MCA).

A list of clothing supplied to the Marine Guard aboard the *Constitution* dated April 20, 1798, included "300 blue under Jackets [vests] with sleeves," which may have been for fatigue duty. Included in the same list was "180 blue outside Jackets." For use in cold weather and sentry duty, this was

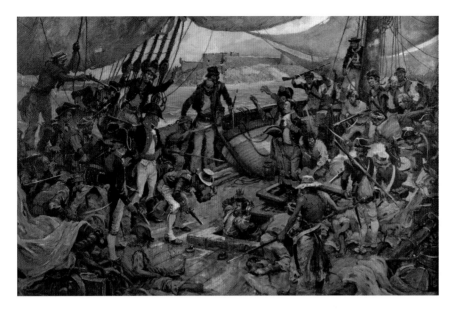

probably the garment referred to as a "Watch Coat" in the 1804 Regulations (PWD 1798: xlg21). Writing to Agent Stephen Higginson on December 29, 1798, Burrows advised that one watch coat was prescribed for every two Marines (MCA).

Duty in the West Indian tropics made it essential that Marines wore a lightweight uniform. According to a letter from Burrows to Clinch dated March 3, 1800, this was to be made of white "Russia Duck" and the coat had to be "lapelled, have a red cape, two buttons on each side the lapells and have a short skirt. The whole to be bound with Red Ferret [tape]" (MCA). Pantaloons were also to be edged with scarlet tape. Some officers drew alternative warm-weather clothing for their detachments. On January 8, 1800, Strother, aboard the frigate USS *Congress*, informed Burrows, "I had drawn … sixty frocks calculated for the climate we have to serve in" (MCA). Officers serving in hot climates were directed to wear an undress linen coatee similar to that acquired for enlisted men.

From 1797 to 1801 Marines were armed with 1794 contract .69-caliber "Charleville" French-pattern muskets made by US contractors primarily using salvaged French musket parts drawn from US storage depots. In 1801 these muskets began to be replaced by British .76-caliber Model 1793 India Pattern muskets, which remained in use until 1827. As the British muskets were of a larger bore, the Marine Corps does not appear to have adopted the Army's Model 1808 accouterments.

The Army-pattern cartridge box used with the 1794 contract musket was of the same pattern as used during the American Revolutionary War, and was suspended from a black leather shoulder sling, with a wooden block bored with about 24 holes to accommodate paper cartridges. The Army-pattern cartridge box was replaced after 1801 by an improved box to accommodate India Pattern musket cartridges; this had a tin compartment underneath the block containing another 11 rounds and spare flints, plus a pocket at the front for oilcloth, worm, and screwdriver. According to a receipt from John Harris, Military Store Keeper at Philadelphia, Army-pattern painted knapsacks were issued to the Marine Guard aboard the *United States* on March 3, 1798 (NRC – entry 377).

THE FIRST BARBARY WAR

About a year after the ending of hostilities with France on September 30, 1800, the United States became embroiled in the First Barbary War (1801–05) in the Mediterranean. For years, pirates or corsairs from the Barbary Coast of Algeria, Morocco, Tripoli, Tunis, and Algiers had been seizing American merchant ships and holding the crews for ransom, demanding the United States pay tribute to the Barbary rulers to prevent further attacks.

By 1801 the United States was paying a tribute amounting to more than two million dollars a year – a sum more than one-fifth of its annual federal revenue. During that year Yusuf Karamanli, the Pasha of Tripoli, demanded a further $225,000, but newly elected President Thomas Jefferson refused to pay. In response, Karamanli declared war on the United States by ordering the cutting down of the flagstaff in front of the American consulate in Tripoli on May 14, 1801 (*NI & WA*, Jan. 6, 1802: 2.4).

Numerous small amphibious landings and ferocious sea-fights involving Marines took place during the ensuing conflict. On August 1, 1801, the schooner USS *Enterprise*, commanded by First Lieutenant Andrew Sterret, defeated the 14-gun Tripolitan polacca *Tripoli* after a three-hour battle at close quarters in the Mediterranean Sea. The role of the sea soldiers aboard the *Enterprise* in repelling boarders and delivering lethal musket fire were important factors in victory. According to an American newspaper report, "owing to the nearness of the vessels which were within pistol shot of each other [the Marines] were eminently useful" (*NI & WA*, Nov. 18, 1801: 3.1). While there were no American casualties, the Tripolitans suffered 20 killed and 30 wounded.

On October 31, 1803, the Tripolitan navy captured USS *Philadelphia* intact after the frigate ran aground on an uncharted coral reef about 5 miles east of Tripoli. Efforts by the Americans to refloat *Philadelphia* while under fire from shore batteries and enemy vessels failed and the ship was captured (*CDC*, Mar. 26, 1804: 2.1). The crew, including Commodore William Bainbridge, were taken ashore and held as hostages, while *Philadelphia* was anchored in Tripoli harbor as a gun battery. On the evening of February 16, 1804, First Lieutenant Stephen Decatur entered the harbor with 80 volunteers, including a seven-man detachment of Marines under Sergeant Solomon Wren, hidden aboard the captured Tripolitan ketch *Mastico* (later renamed USS *Intrepid*.) Quietly drawing alongside *Philadelphia* undetected, Decatur's boarding party took the Tripolitan ship's guard completely by surprise and set fire to the stricken frigate, which was soon a blazing inferno, thus denying it further use by the enemy. Decatur's men next made their escape in *Mastico* with only one man wounded, and rowed beyond the reach of the shore batteries before the Tripolitans fully realized what had happened (McClellan 1925: 1.15.18).

On August 3, 1804, the US Navy squadron commanded by Commodore Edward Preble bombarded Tripoli while smaller gunboats engaged enemy vessels in the harbor. When nine men from Gunboat No. 6, which included Marines, led by Acting Lieutenant John Trippe boarded a Tripolitan gunboat, the sea washing between the two vessels caused their separation before the rest of the boarding party could follow. Finding themselves isolated and outnumbered five to one, the boarders engaged in a fierce hand-to-hand fight during which Trippe was severely wounded by multiple saber cuts.

"The Assault on Derna," painted by Colonel Charles H. Waterhouse, USMCR (Ret.), depicts the moment First Lieutenant Presley N. O'Bannon and his squad of Marines helped capture the Tripolitan fortress at Derna on April 27, 1805. The US flotilla, consisting of the brig *Argus*, schooner *Nautilus*, and sloop *Hornet*, can be seen in the background bombarding the fortress. (Art Collection, National Museum of the Marine Corps: Accession Number: 29-454)

Coming to his rescue, Sergeant Johnathan Meredith USMC bayoneted his assailant, pinning him to the deck. Four days later Meredith was killed in the explosion of Gunboat No. 3 during a similar attack on the Tripolitans (McClellan 1925: 1.15.19–20).

One of the most outstanding actions of the First Barbary War was the American-led overland campaign against the fortress at Derna. A force of about 500 Arab and Greek mercenaries under the putative command of Hamet Karamanli, the Pasha of Tripoli's exiled older brother, set out from Alexandria on a 600-mile trek across the desert to Derna on March 8, 1805. Raised and led by William H. Eaton, Navy Agent for the Barbary Regencies, they were accompanied by a squad of seven US Marines under First Lieutenant Presley N. O'Bannon, off the brig USS *Argus* (McClellan 1925: 1.15.27). Eaton's originally request for 100 Marines had been refused. Transportation consisted of 107 camels and a few asses.

On January 11, 1805, while the Americans were in Cairo planning the campaign, Muhammad Ali, Viceroy of Egypt, presented O'Bannon, plus Navy Master Commandant Isaac Hull, commander of *Argus*, and Midshipman George Mann, with an Arab, or "Mameluke," scimitar with shamshir, or curved, blade (Cureton 2006: 121 & 123).

During the march in torturous heat to Derna, Eaton faced several rebellions among the mercenaries, which were quelled thanks to the stern action of O'Bannon's Marines. Running out of food, the expedition slaughtered and ate some of their camels. Finally reaching Bomba, about 20 miles from Derna, on April 15, the column was reprovisioned and drew munitions from the *Argus* and the sloop USS *Hornet* in preparation for the assault.

Arriving in front of the fortress at Derna on April 26, Eaton offered terms of surrender to Mustafa Bey, the Governor of Derna, on condition that he swore allegiance to Hamet Karamanli, to which the Bey replied, "My head or yours!" (quoted in Prentiss 1813: 337). The assault on the fortress commenced at 1400hrs the next day in conjunction with the bombarding guns of *Argus* and *Hornet*, and the schooner USS *Nautilus*.

Prior to the assault, two small "field-pieces" for the use of Eaton's force were rowed ashore from *Nautilus*. The steepness of the cliffs permitted only one of these guns to be hoisted ashore, however, and this was quickly mounted on its carriage and made ready for action. The guns in the fortress kept up a heavy fire, but fell silent after about an hour of shelling from sea and land, following which they were abandoned as the Tripolitan garrison took shelter in the town and surrounding buildings. The naval guns were next turned on the beach and kept up a heavy fire to clear the way for the final assault.

Ordering a charge, Eaton was joined by the detachment of Marines plus a mixed force of Arab cannoneers and Greek militia, all under immediate command of O'Bannon. As they rushed toward what remained of the Tripolitan defenses, 14 of O'Bannon's force were killed or wounded. Among the former was Marine Private John Whilton. Marine Private Edward Steward was seriously wounded and died three days later. Also among the wounded were Privates David Thomas and Bernard O'Brien, plus Eaton who received a musket ball through his wrist (*KG*, Oct. 1, 1805: 3.2). Observing events from *Argus*, Hull wrote:

> At about half past 3 we had the satisfaction to see Lieut. O'Bannen [*sic*] of the marine corps, and Mr. Mann, midshipman of the Argus, with a few brave fellows with them, enter the fort, haul down the enemy's flag and plant the American ensign on the walls of the battery … Whilst our men were turning the guns of the battery on the town, Hamet Bashaw had taken possession of the back part of it, which brought the enemy betwixt two fires, that soon silenced them, and about 4 in the afternoon we had complete possession of the town and fort … (*MG*, Oct. 31, 1805: 2.2)

As a result of this action, O'Bannon had the honor of being the first American officer to hoist the "Stars and Stripes" flag over a captured citadel in the "Old World." Eaton's force next held Derna against a Tripolitan army until June 1805, when they learned that the United States had negotiated a peace treaty with Yusuf Karamanli. Likely disappointed in their endeavors, what remained of the Marine detachment eventually evacuated the fort and re-joined their vessel.

Upon return to the United States in 1806, O'Bannon was presented in honor of his exploits in North Africa with a sword with a silver eagle-head hilt, and British Model 1796 light cavalry-pattern blade with on one side the inscription "Presented by the State of Virginia to her gallant son, Priestly [*sic*] N. O'Bannon," and on the other "Assault and Conquest of the City of Derne in Africa, April 27, 1805." As a further consequence of O'Bannon's success in 1805, the Colors carried by the Marine Corps were later inscribed with the words, "To the Shores of Tripoli."

Uniform, arms, and equipment 1804–21

The first printed order for a new Marine Corps uniform introduced in 1804 was published on October 14, 1805. To bring together all the minor changes in this uniform that occurred during the next five years, a Formal Order was issued by Secretary of the Navy Paul Hamilton on April 19, 1810 (McClellan 1925: 1.18.42–43, fn. 77). The introduction of this uniform for enlisted men was slow as stores of the old uniform had to be used up before

the 1804-pattern uniform could be issued, although officers were advised to encourage their men to purchase the new coat with their meager pay.

Officers wore a dark-blue coatee with scarlet facings on collar and cuffs, buttoned across the breast with two rows of eight buttons connected by a herringbone pattern of gold lace with square-shaped points at either end and brought to a shallow "V" shape at the center. Similarly, the lower sleeves and coat tails had three buttons at the center of three strips of "V"-shaped gold lace with square-shaped points. The collar had two blind gold-lace buttonholes either side. Scarlet "turnbacks" were sewn on the coat tails. A gold-thread foul anchor at the bottom of each skirt was replaced by a gold-lace diamond on a blue ground in 1809 (McClellan 1925: 1.18.41, fn. 77). Drop-front pantaloons were white and fastened with small buttons.

A cocked hat, or *chapeau-bras*, had a scarlet plume, and a gold-lace loop with a US Navy button under a black silk cockade. Summer headgear consisted of a "round hat" with a gold band and tassel, which was abandoned in 1809 (McClellan 1925: 1.18.41, fn. 77). Hair was still queued and powdered. Footwear consisted of knee-high black leather boots.

Born in Fauquier County, Virginia, in 1776, Presley N. O'Bannon, depicted here as a first lieutenant, entered the US Marine Corps as a second lieutenant on January 18, 1801. The dark or black facings on the collar and cuffs of his coat are at odds with the 1804 Regulations and should be scarlet. Promoted to first lieutenant on October 15, 1802, he was assigned to the brig USS *Argus* and won fame for bravery in action serving under diplomatic Consul General William H. Eaton during the Tripoli campaign in 1805. Upon his return to the United States the next year, O'Bannon was presented with a sword with a silver eagle-head hilt and a curved blade modeled after the original Mameluke sword presented to him by Hamet Karamanli in honor of his exploits in North Africa. Resigning from the US Navy on March 6, 1807, O'Bannon settled in Russellville, Logan County, Kentucky, and served in the Kentucky State Legislature and militia; he died on September 2, 1850, in Pleasureville, Kentucky, aged 74. Painting by Colonel Donald L. Dickson, USMCR. (Art Collection, National Museum of the Marine Corps: Accession Number: 32-2-50)

Rank insignia for colonel was a gold epaulet on each shoulder; major, the same; captain, a gold epaulet on the right shoulder and a gold counter-strap, or epaulet without fringe, on the left shoulder. When in command of a ship's guard, a first or senior lieutenant wore a gold epaulet on the right shoulder, but had to move it to the left shoulder once his command was over. Staff officers wore a gold epaulet and gold-edged blue cloth counter-strap without fringe. When on duty officers wore a scarlet waist sash tied on the left side. A shoulder belt of whitened buff leather, with oval brass breast plate, supported a sword with brass-mounted scabbard.

Enlisted Marines wore a dark-blue single-breasted coatee, with scarlet collar, cuffs, shoulder straps, and "turnbacks," fastened by eight Navy foul anchor buttons, with yellow lace on each side of the chest forming a shallow "V" shape.

Sergeants wore fringed yellow worsted straps on each shoulder. In 1821, heavily padded yellow wings replaced scarlet-trimmed shoulder straps for enlisted men. As a result, those clothiers fulfilling Marine Corps contracts had to supply "Uniform Coats with the wings fitted on" (*DNI*, Oct. 9, 1822:

3.4). Pantaloons were plain white, wool in winter and linen in summer. Black cloth gaiters fastened with small yellow-metal buttons came up to the calf of the leg. On October 21, 1806, newly issued gaiters were to reach the knee.

Headgear consisted of a high-crowned felt and leather cap with brass plate, plus cap band and tassel of yellow worsted, which had been changed from a combination of dark blue, yellow, and red on July 7, 1806. Sergeants wore a leather cockade and 5in-tall scarlet feather plume on the left side of the cap. Other enlisted men wore a scarlet plush worsted plume of the same height on the front of the cap. On April 3, 1818, Lieutenant Colonel Commandant Franklin Wharton informed John Bullus, Navy Agent at New York that "One hundred uniform caps of a new pattern" had been made for the Marine Corps by Robert Dingee, the most prominent supplier of leather items to the US military during the first half of the 19th century (MCA).

Musicians wore a coatee of scarlet cloth with white facings, with the same cut and trimming as NCOs and privates. On October 21, 1806, they were instructed to wear a scarlet feather plume rather than a pompon on the dress cap (Naval Records).

The white summer dress adopted in 1800 was discontinued after April 14, 1804, on which date Wharton informed First Lieutenant Anthony Cale at Philadelphia, "The white coats for Officers, as well as men are done away with" (MCA).

Although the 1804 Regulations offered no information about fatigue clothing for enlisted men, the supply of which began soon after March 27, 1804, Inspector of Marines Major Samuel Miller invited proposals for "1000 Fatigue Jackets [and] Trowsers" of "Dark Mixed" on January 7, 1820 (*DNI*,

This Pattern 1810 epaulet was worn for full dress by a field-grade Marine officer. It consists of a strap with oval-shaped shoulder pad covered in gold lace. The bullion-covered crescent is edged with gold cord. The gold-bullion fringe is ½in in diameter and 3½in in length. A button through the opening on the strap secured it to the coat near the collar. Tie strings went through eyelets on the shoulder and tied inside the coat near the shoulder seam. (National Museum of the Marine Corps: Accession No. 1975.637.1)

Jan. 7, 1820: 3.4). In response, ten days later New York clothier Stephen Lester submitted an estimate to supply the Marine Corps with 1,000 each of plain, unlaced fatigue jackets and trousers of "gray mixed cloth" (MCA). On November 4 of the same year, Miller required 938 "gray Kersey Fatigue Jackets ... [and] Overalls" (CWG, Nov. 4, 1820: 3.4).

The issuance of undress headgear consisting of a leather foraging cap began in 1811. Also referred to as "Glazed Caps," these were unsatisfactory, being liable to crack and, according to Lieutenant Colonel Commandant Anthony Gale, "got so soft" that they looked "bad" (MCA). These began to be replaced in 1819 by cloth caps with leather tops, which were probably precursors of the wide-topped Pattern 1825 shakos that had worsted cords radiating from a military button on the cap top.

On January 7, 1820, Miller invited proposals for the supply of "60 watch coats, of dark mixt [sic] cloth," (DNI, Jan. 15, 1820: 1.2) and on January 24 clothier Nathaniel Kimball, of Georgetown, DC, supplied Miller with watch coats of "gray mixed cloth" (MCA). A few watch coats were issued to each unit for use by sentries in inclement weather.

Regarding accouterments for enlisted Marines, a Bill published in 1808 listing items in store included 306 each of "Knapsacks," "Cartouch boxes, belts and scabbards," and "Flint, brushes and prickers" (AC, Dec. 20, 1808: 2.3). The belts referred to were whitened buff leather. Worn over both shoulders they supported a cartridge box and bayonet scabbard. According to a letter to Wharton from First Lieutenant Samuel B. Johnston, commanding the brig USS Niagara, cartridge boxes carried by Marines had a small plate attached to the outer flap (MCA).

THE WAR OF 1812

After ten years of tension and rivalry on the High Seas, the United States went to war again with Great Britain in June 1812. By this time the still much-reduced US Marine Corps consisted of only ten officers and 483 enlisted men, while the US Navy had a mere 16 vessels on its list. Nevertheless, the Marines continued to distinguish themselves on both land and at sea. Writing to a friend after being appointed to command the Marine detachment on board Captain Isaac Hull's Constitution, First Lieutenant William S. Bush declared, "Should an opportunity be afforded for boarding the enemy, I will be the first man upon his deck" (The Port Folio, 1813: 15). On August 19, 1812, Bush's wish came true when his ship engaged the British frigate HMS Guerriere in the North Atlantic approximately 400 miles southeast of Halifax, Nova Scotia. As the vessels hove together at close quarters, Bush leapt to the taffrail, and is reputed to have called out to Hull, "Shall I board her, Sir?" and was promptly shot dead by a Royal Marine whose musket ball struck Bush on his left cheekbone and passed through to the back of his head. Undeterred, the Marine marksmen in Constitution's tops swept Guerriere's decks and did much to bring about the final surrender of the first British man-of-war since the American Revolutionary War. When news of Bush's death reached Washington on October 19, 1812, Lieutenant Colonel Commandant Wharton ordered all officers to wear black crepe on the left arm and sword hilt for one month. Furthermore, Bush's nearest male relative, nephew

Lewis B. Jackson, received a posthumous silver medal from Congress in early 1835 in honor of his uncle's bravery.

During the epic cruise in 1813–14 of the 32-gun frigate USS *Essex*, commanded by Captain David Porter, against the British whaling fleet in the Pacific, Second Lieutenant John M. Gamble had the honor of being the only Marine officer ever to command a ship. With two experienced sailors as mates, Gamble was appointed prize-master of the sloop-of-war *Greenwich*, a British vessel captured off the Galapagos Islands in the Southern Pacific during May 1813. Operating within a flotilla of captured ships under Porter, *Greenwich* chased and captured the whaler *Seringapatam* on July 14, for which Gamble, *Greenwich*'s Marine commander, was greatly praised. On November 19, Porter's flotilla of prizes put in at Nuka Hiva, the largest island in the Marquesas Islands, which they named Massachusetts Bay. Departing for Valparaíso, Chile, on December 9, Porter left Gamble to make repairs to his own vessel plus *Seringapatam* and *Sir Andrew Hammond*, another captured whaler. If the *Essex* had not returned within three or four months, Gamble was under instructions to also sail the flotilla for Valparaíso.

With no sign of Porter's return by early summer of 1814, the men under Gamble's command grew restless. On May 7, a mutiny occurred on the *Seringapatam* during which Gamble was wounded, following which the mutineers sailed off in the whaler. To make matters worse, as the remainder of the men under the command of the wounded Marine officer made preparations to set out for Valparaíso, the indigenous inhabitants of Nuka Hiva attacked, killing three sailors and seriously wounding one Marine. Burning the *Greenwich*, Gamble set sail in *Sir Andrew Hammond*. Believing he could not reach the Chilean coast, he steered for the Sandwich Islands and after further hardships and narrow escapes from shipwreck was captured on June 11, 1814, by the British sloop HMS *Cherub*, and taken into Rio de Janeiro, Brazil, about nine months later. With news of peace between the United States and Britain, Gamble finally made it back to New York City via a Swedish ship that transferred him to an American vessel, toward the end of August 1815, following which he was promoted to the rank of captain (*VA*, Sep. 6, 1815: 3.3).

One of the finest hours at sea for the Marines during the War of 1812 came in defeat. In an action off Boston on June 1, 1813, the frigate USS *Chesapeake*, commanded by Captain James Lawrence, was disabled by the guns of Captain Philip Broke's frigate HMS *Shannon*. As the two ships closed, Lawrence was mortally wounded by a musket ball fired by Lieutenant John Law of the Royal Marines. As Lawrence uttered his last words, "Don't give up the ship!" a British boarding party hacked its way on to *Chesapeake*'s quarterdeck to be met by her Marine guard under First Lieutenant James Broome, which put up a stubborn resistance. During this action Broome was severely wounded, having his head "cut from the top to near his mouth by the ear," while his Marines fought valiantly. Of their original number of 44 men, 12 including their commanding officer were killed, and 20 were wounded (*CC*, Jul. 5, 1813: 2.4).

Several months later, on August 12, Commodore Oliver H. Perry's flagship the brig USS *Lawrence*, named in honor of the fallen Lawrence, flew from her masthead a blue battle flag crudely lettered with "Don't give up the Ship" when he met with a more heavily armed British squadron of six ships on the waters of Lake Erie on September 10, 1813 (*USG*, Oct. 20, 1813: 4.4). During the fight, Perry's Marine officer, Second Lieutenant John Brooks, Jr., son of the Governor of Massachusetts, was badly wounded in the hip and bled to death, but the victorious Perry was eventually able to report, "We have met the enemy and they are ours: two ships, two brigs, one schooner, and one sloop" (Jackson 1840: 52). Perry received a gold medal and thanks from Congress for the victory.

In the failed American attempt to protect the District of Columbia and capital at Washington from attack by British forces under Major-General Robert Ross during the battle of Bladensburg on August 24, 1814, a party of seamen, or "flotilla men," serving five guns under Commodore Joshua Barney and supported by a Marine battalion of 103 officers and

Marines in Pattern 1804 dress uniform man the rigging of the sloop-of-war USS *Wasp* (not to be confused with the earlier schooner of the same name) during the action against the British 18-gun brig-sloop HMS *Reindeer* on June 28, 1814. *Wasp*, under Master Commandant Johnston Blakely, captured six prizes in the approaches to the English Channel before the smaller *Reindeer* closed with the US ship. Musket balls from 26 Marines in the tops of *Wasp* made short work of the British, killing and wounding 67 of the crew. After burning *Reindeer*, Blakely took his ship into a French port to refit. *Wasp* went back into action at the end of August 1814 and continued to wreak havoc on British shipping until later that year the ship disappeared at sea, apparently lost in a storm. Painting by Sergeant John F. Clymer. (Art Collection, National Museum of the Marine Corps, Acc. No. 1976.386.1)

men commanded by Captain Samuel Miller, was the last unit to fall back in the face of the onslaught of British light infantry. Barney's force took up position on the turnpike about 1 mile from the Eastern Branch of the Potomac River with two 18-pounder guns served by sailors on the road, and three 12-pounders on the right manned by sailors and Marines, with the remainder of the Marine battalion plus armed sailors as infantry support. Having failed to make a frontal assault along the pike, Ross ordered an attack across a field on the right flank of Barney's position about noon. As American forces withdrew in disorder, Barney failed to receive the order to fall back, although the ammunition wagon serving his guns did withdraw. With the sailors and Marines surrounded and overrun, Barney received a severe wound in the thigh, and Miller was badly wounded in the arm. With command handed to Captain Alexander Sevier, who was himself wounded in the neck, the remainder of the Marines, plus sailors, were ordered in full retreat. The Marines sustained 21 casualties including eight killed (Wilkinson 1816: 788). Barney and Miller were captured and exchanged soon after.

Both Miller and Sevier were awarded the brevet rank of major for "gallantry and good conduct" at Bladensburg in December 1814 (*LL*, Dec. 10, 1814: 3.1). A British officer writing after the battle about the fighting qualities of the American Marines and sailors, observed that "not only did they serve their guns with quickness and precision which astonished their assailants, but they stood till some of them were actually bayoneted, with fuses in their hands; nor was it till … they saw themselves deserted on all sides by the soldiers that they quitted the field" (Clowes 1897: 146).

Three weeks after the action at Bladensburg, about 200 Marines were involved in the defense of Baltimore and Fort McHenry, Maryland, during September 12–15, 1814. A small detachment of Marines helped man several batteries on Hampstead or Loudenslager Hill, to the east of the city. The Marines off *Guerriere* under First Lieutenant Joseph L. Kuhn were posted in the entrenchments in support of two batteries defending the road leading into the city from Sparrow's Point (*NWR*, Vol. VII, September 1814–March 1815: 156).

Entitled "Repulse of the Highlanders," this dramatic painting by Colonel Charles H. Waterhouse, USMCR (Ret.), depicts the attack on the American parapet after the British capture of the advance redoubt next to the riverbank at New Orleans on January 8, 1815. Wearing the uniform formally prescribed by the 1810 Regulations, the Marines repulse elements of the 93rd (Sutherland Highlanders) Regiment of Foot. According to an officer of the 93rd, the advance of his regiment was halted by heavy artillery and musketry fire and, far from engaging in hand-to-hand combat, his men did not see a single American soldier during the action because the defenders kept discharging their weapons without lifting their faces above the ramparts. (Art Collection, National Museum of the Marine Corps: Accession No. 29-452)

After the failure of the British land attack and withdrawal of the Royal Navy fleet after its 24-hour bombardment, these Marines were among thousands of American military and citizens who witnessed the raising of a large garrison-size "Stars and Stripes" flag over Fort McHenry, which signaled the American victory. This action inspired a prominent Washington lawyer, Francis S. Key, to write a poem the words of which were used for the song "The Star Spangled Banner," which eventually became the official national anthem of the United States in 1931.

Following an unsuccessful attempt to capture Mobile, Alabama, in September 1814, the British began their assault on New Orleans on December 14, 1814, which ended with an American victory on January 8, 1815. Meanwhile hostilities were officially concluded with the signing of the Peace of Ghent, in the United Netherlands, on December 24, 1814. Unaware of this, Major-General Sir Edward Pakenham boasted that he would eat Christmas dinner in New Orleans after capturing the city. The initial British advance involved the transportation of about 1,000 sailors and Marines, under Royal Navy Captain Nicholas Lockyer, across Lake Borgne in 42

C MARINES AT NEW ORLEANS, 1814

Accompanying artillery, Marines uniformed according to the 1804 Regulations, which were formalized in 1810, charge to drive off British infantry at New Orleans on December 23, 1814.

Urging his men on, the first lieutenant (**1**) wears a *chapeau* with scarlet plume and gold-lace loop with a US Navy button under a black silk cockade. His double-breasted coat has scarlet facings on the collar and cuffs, and "V"-shaped herringbone-pattern gold lace across the chest. His fall-front white linen pantaloons are fastened with small yellow US Navy buttons. Rank is indicated by a gold epaulet on his left shoulder, and a crimson waist sash. His footwear consists of knee-high black leather boots.

Charging with fixed bayonet, the sergeant (**2**) wears a high-crowned felt-and-leather cap with brass plate, tall scarlet feathered plume, and leather cockade on the left side, and a cap band and tassel of yellow worsted. His rank is also indicated by a fringed yellow worsted strap on each shoulder. His coat has a plain scarlet collar and cuffs, sewn-down scarlet "turnbacks," and yellow worsted chest braid. His black linen gaiters are fastened with small metal buttons, and his shoes have yellow-metal buckles. He is armed with a .76-caliber Model 1793 India Pattern musket. Accouterments are a Pattern 1808 cartridge box and leather scabbard with brass mounts, both of which are attached to whitened buff leather shoulder belts.

The private (**3**) wears the same pattern of uniform minus rank indicators, and has a worsted scarlet plume at the front of his shako. He carries the same weapon type, and has a Lherbette-pattern cotton duck canvas knapsack.

barges. This attack was slowed due to the action of five US Navy gunboats commanded by Lieutenant Thomas ap Catesby Jones USN. Although all the gunboats were captured, their action gave Brevet Major General Andrew Jackson much-needed time to strengthen the defenses at New Orleans.

Pakenham next sent a brigade under Major-General John Keane across Lake Borgne to establish an encampment with its left flank on the Mississippi River. On the evening of December 23, troops directly under Jackson's command attacked Keane's brigade with a force of 1,500 men, among whom was a battalion temporarily commanded by Major Daniel Carmick composed of a 56-man company of Marines plus Major Jean Baptiste Plauché's four-company battalion of Creole volunteers. The Marines were under the immediate command of First Lieutenant François-Godefroy Barbin de Bellevue, a New Orleans Creole who had been commissioned in the US Marine Corps in 1812. During this action they prevented the capture of a battery with a loss of eight killed and eight wounded. After disrupting Keane's brigade, Jackson ordered his troops to fall back behind the Rodriguez Canal, with their left flank on the Mississippi and the right flank secured by a cypress swamp.

During Pakenham's first attack on Jackson's line, which began on December 28, Carmick remained in command of Plauché's battalion, which formed part of Jackson's right flank. Meanwhile, the 24-gun sloop USS Louisiana took station across the Mississippi from Jackson's line so as to enfilade his front. The Marine guard aboard Louisiana was commanded by 30-year-old Second Lieutenant John R. Montegut, the son of a prominent New Orleans surgeon. The guns of Louisiana opened up with telling effect on the two advancing British columns. The column on the left, nearest the Mississippi, halted about 600yd from the American line in the face of a galling fire that was mostly from Louisiana, as Jackson had only five guns on that part of his front. Meanwhile, the British right-hand column nearest the cypress swamp moved out of range of Louisiana but, without artillery support, Pakenham was reluctant to advance any farther and withdrew both columns to a position about 2 miles from the American line.

Of about 5,500 British troops in action that day, Pakenham lost about 45 killed and wounded. Jackson lost only seven killed and eight wounded, of 3,282 Americans present (HC, Feb. 21, 1815: 2.4). Among the latter was Carmick, who was wounded three times while delivering an order to Plauché. Already struck by a ball through his right arm, and suffering the loss of his right thumb, which was carried away by grapeshot, his horse was hit by a Congreve rocket that also wounded Carmick in the head (USG, Feb. 8, 1815: 3.5).

The stricken Carmick was taken to a city hospital and was presumably still there at the time of Pakenham's second and climatic attack on January 8, 1815. On that occasion, Marines and sailors from the destroyed schooner USS Carolina manned Batteries Nos 2 and 4 on the right wing of Jackson's line. The 66-man company commanded by Bellevue was posted at the center and to the right of Battery No. 7 (Upton 1904: 134–35). The musketry of Bellevue's company did much to repel the advance of the main British column, and Pakenham fell at a spot about 200yd from the American line and about 400yd in a 45-degree left-oblique direction from the position of the Marines. In this decisive American victory, the overall British loss was about 2,000 killed and wounded, compared to American losses of only seven killed and six wounded.

NEW CHALLENGES 1815–35

Although the Marines had fought bravely during the War of 1812, the Corps' record was tarnished by scandal. Appointed to command the Corps on March 7, 1804, Lieutenant Colonel Franklin Wharton was berated by fellow Marine officers for his failure to review or inspect the Marines, or command them in the field. Instead of fighting the British when they raided Washington in 1814, Wharton was accused of fleeing the Marine Barracks as the capital burned. During that raid, he gathered the remnants of his headquarters, the band, and the clerks with their records, and marched to the Navy Yard. Although instructed by Secretary of the Navy William Jones to rally with the rest of the government at Frederick, Maryland, Wharton asked the yard commandant, Captain Thomas Tingey USN, if he wanted the Marines to help either defend or destroy the yard. In response, Tingey told him to leave because the British were near the city and the yard was ready to be burned. Thus, Wharton and his Marines left by a small boat.

Despite the scandal caused by his failure to defend the capital in 1814, Lieutenant Colonel Franklin Wharton, the third Commandant of the US Marine Corps, made a substantial contribution to the organization and its efficient running. Under his guidance, its uniforms and military equipment were for the first time standardized, and uniform military practices were established throughout the service. (Art Collection, National Museum of the Marine Corps: Accession No. psuLqL4g)

Archibald Henderson, the fifth Commandant of the US Marine Corps, served for 39 years from 1820 through 1859, and did more than any other individual to form the character of the Marine Corps. He fought aboard *Constitution* in 1815, and eventually became known as "the Grand Old Man" of the Marine Corps. (Art Collection, National Museum of the Marine Corps, Triangle, Virginia. Acc. No. 1975.663.1)

Some Marine officers far from the scene – including Archibald Henderson, who was commissioned a second lieutenant in the US Marine Corps in 1806 and served aboard *Constitution* during its famous victories in the War of 1812 – thought that Wharton had damaged the fighting fame of the Marine Corps by not taking the field himself. In 1817, Wharton faced a court-martial for "Neglect of Duty," and "Conduct Unbecoming of an Officer and a Gentleman," because he called a former Marine major a liar, but was acquitted of all charges (*BDA*, Oct. 13, 1817: 2.2). Urged by President James Monroe to resign, he doggedly maintained his post until his death on September 1, 1818 (*CWG*, Sep. 4, 1818: 4.4). Wharton's successor as Marine Commandant, Major Anthony Gale, was cashiered for drunkenness after only two years in office. On October 17, 1820, Brevet Major Archibald Henderson was appointed the fifth Commandant of the Marines.

During the next 12 years, Marine Corps detachments were involved as the US Navy chased pirates in the Caribbean, and showed the "Stars and Stripes" flag everywhere from Sumatra to the Falkland Islands. It was at home, however, that the Marine Corps encountered its next serious enemy. On December 8, 1829, President Andrew Jackson created consternation throughout its ranks by a recommendation to merge the Marines into "the artillery or infantry," based on the belief that "no peculiar training" was required for Marine Corps service. A bitter debate dragged on for several years, during which US Navy Master Commandant David Conner supported Jackson by successfully completing a cruise in the sloop-of-war USS *Erie* without a Marine guard. The Military Affairs Committee in the House of Representatives ruled it was out of order to interfere with the status of the Marine Corps, however, and finally Congress passed "An Act for the Better Organization of the Marine Corps" on June 30, 1834. As a result, the Marines were not only saved but increased to an unprecedented peacetime strength of 63 officers and 1,224 enlisted men. Furthermore, Henderson was promoted to the rank of colonel.

Uniform, arms, and equipment 1821–34

The 1821 Regulations formalized minor uniform changes, which resulted in three slightly different patterns of uniform dress. Field-grade officers and captains continued to wear the Pattern 1804 double-breasted coatee with square-shaped points on chest and sleeve lace. Lieutenants wore single-breasted coatees with lozenge-shaped loops on chest and sleeve lace. Enlisted Marines wore bastion-shaped loops on chest and sleeve lace. Gold binding was added around the scarlet collar for all ranks, and the skirts of the coatee

Nord-Amerikanische Armee. Marine Infanterie.

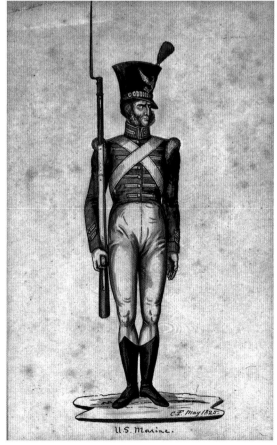

C.F. May 1825.

U.S. Marine.

were rounded in cut. Epaulets continued to designate the rank of field-grade officers and captains, while lieutenants wore the coatee with wings and indicated rank with sleeve chevrons.

A more fully prescribed undress uniform for Marine officers was also introduced. The dark-blue coatee worn by the Lieutenant Colonel Commandant had a single row of ten Marine buttons, with four of the same pattern on both cuffs and the skirts. All company-grade officers' coatees had a nine-button front, and four buttons on each cuff and the skirts, with the exception of first and second lieutenants' coatees, which had three buttons on the skirts.

Dark-blue pantaloons were prescribed for winter and white for summer. For headgear, from January 1, 1824, all company-grade officers, NCOs, musicians, and privates wore a bell-crown shako for uniform dress (Order of Henderson, Nov. 27, 1823, MCA).

For full dress, officers wore a 2in-wide white leather sword belt over a scarlet silk net sash. Influenced by the exploits of First Lieutenant Presley N. O'Bannon during the First Barbary War in 1805, in April 1825, Lieutenant Colonel Commandant Henderson ordered all Marine officers to carry what became the Model 1826 Marine officer's sword with "Mameluke" hilt. This sword pattern was prescribed until 1859 when it was replaced by the Army's Model 1850 foot-officer's sword. With the exception of the years 1859–75

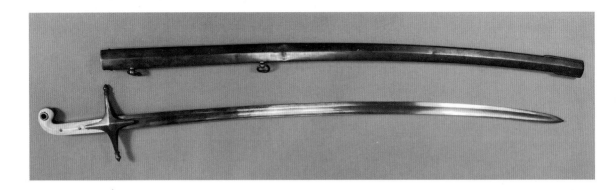

In 1826, a sword with a hilt patterned after the scimitar presented by Muhammad Ali, Viceroy of Egypt, to First Lieutenant Presley N. O'Bannon, was introduced for all US Marine Corps officers. Abandoned in 1859 for the heavier US Army foot-officer's sword with metal guard and wire-wrapped leather grip, the "Mameluke" pattern was reintroduced in 1875. With an ivory grip, brass cross-guard, and brass scabbard, this example was carried by Second Lieutenant Thomas Y. Field, who was commissioned on March 3, 1847, and served in Mexico with the First Marine Battalion, and with Co. E when the unit was reorganized into the Marine Battalion. Promoted to first lieutenant on October 15, 1854, Field rose to the rank of colonel by 1880. (National Museum of the Marine Corps. Accession No. 2008.3.51)

and World War II, "Mameluke"-hilted swords have continued to be carried by Marine Corps officers for full dress and service dress on special occasions. When on duty in undress, all officers carried their sword on a black leather shoulder belt, which was discontinued in 1825 and replaced by a waist belt with yellow mountings.

During the mid-1820s the yellow lace on enlisted men's blue coats followed the design of officers' coats with bastion-shaped points at each end of the herringbone braid, and the same on the collar and lower sleeves. Enlisted men's shoulder wings also became more elaborate with yellow-trimmed blue straps and buff rolls. Concerning footwear during this period, on October 26, 1824, Quartermaster Elijah J. Weed requested "2100 pairs best quality coarse Shoes" (*ACDA*, Oct. 30, 1824: 3.2).

In 1828 the Marine Corps began to replace the India Pattern British musket with the .69-caliber Model 1816 flintlock musket, at which time Army Pattern 1828 accouterments were adopted. Equipage for enlisted men continued to consist of two whitened buff leather shoulder belts supporting a cartridge box and bayonet scabbard. From July 1828, the bayonet belt had a plain convex brass oval breast plate attached. On May 29, 1824, all enlisted men were also to wear a whitened buff leather waist belt, which was needed to hold the shoulder belts in place when going aloft in a ship's rigging. As such, the Marines were the first US military service to adopt the waist belt for general issue (MCA). Until 1833 this waist belt had a rectangular brass plate with an eagle in the center, after which this was replaced with a plain brass plate.

D **AT MARINE HEADQUARTERS, 1829**

Relocated from Philadelphia to a site near the Navy Yard in Washington, the new Federal capital, in June 1800, the Marine Headquarters forms the background with the Commandant's house on the right.

Standing on the parade ground in winter uniform dress, the first lieutenant (**1**) wears an officers'-pattern bell-crown shako with "eagle" plate and cockade, adopted by the Marine Corps on January 1, 1824. His single-breasted coatee features the alterations introduced in 1821, including lozenge-shaped end loops on the gold chest, collar, and cuff lace, and gold binding around the scarlet collar. Although he has gold wings on both shoulders, rank is indicated by the sleeve chevrons. He carries a Model 1826 Marine officer's sword with "Mameluke" hilt, ivory grip, and gold tassel and knot, in a brass scabbard. His whitened buff leather sword belt with "eagle" plate is fastened over a crimson silk net sash.

In summer uniform dress, the orderly sergeant (**2**) wears an enlisted men's-pattern bell-crown shako. His yellow chest, collar, and cuff lace incorporates bastion-shaped end loops. His wings have yellow-edged blue straps and buff rolls. A single yellow-lace chevron on each sleeve above the elbow indicates his rank. His waist belt plate with "eagle" motif was of the type worn by enlisted Marines from 1828 through 1832. Orderly sergeants were the only NCOs to wear a sash and, as independent commanders of a ship's detachment, were armed with a sword only.

Standing at "Order – Arms," the private (**3**) wears the same pattern of uniform minus chevrons and sash. He is armed with a .69-caliber Model 1816 flintlock musket. His accouterments consist of two whitened buff leather shoulder belts with plain convex brass oval breast plate supporting an Army Pattern 1828 cartridge box and bayonet scabbard.

ABOVE LEFT
Drums with red shells came into use with the Marine Corps in 1834. This example was made by William Ent, of Germantown, Pennsylvania, who made replacement drums for the Marine Corps in 1840 and 1841. (Don Troiani Collection)

ABOVE RIGHT
Blue-shelled drums were adopted by the Marine Corps c.1846, and soon replaced the red-shelled drums. This drum was likely made by William H. Horstmann & Sons of Philadelphia and has painted on the side "Southwark," which was the old name for the Philadelphia Navy Yard area. (Don Troiani Collection)

Uniform, arms, and equipment 1834–41

During his second term in office, which began in 1829, President Andrew Jackson directed that the colors worn by the Continental forces of the American Revolutionary War be restored to the US military. At the same time, Henderson was asked by Secretary of the Navy Levi Woodbury what the Marines wore during that period, to which Henderson advised on March 29, 1833, that officers wore "a green coat faced with white round the cuff." Although he had already proposed a dark-blue, double-breasted uniform coat and matching pants, Henderson conceded that "should it be the wish of the President that the colours worn during that period be adopted – green uniform Coat, similar in form to that at present worn by the Army, with buff facings, gold lace and epaulettes to correspond and light grey pantaloons would perhaps be a uniform even preferable to that recommended" (RG 80, NARA). As a result, Woodbury directed Henderson to propose a uniform based on the latter.

Dated April 2, 1833, the ensuing order was approved by Jackson the next day (RG 127, NARA). The new uniform regulations were formally published for the Marine Corps on April 10, 1833, setting July 4, 1834, as the date when the green uniform would be introduced. It was not until December 7, 1833, however, that Quartermaster Weed issued a request for "Two Thousand Yards of GREEN CLOTH … to be dyed in the wool, in the best indigo or vat blue and weld [a plant the leaves of which produce a bright yellow dye]" (*DNI*, Dec. 20, 1833: 4.2). Furthermore, in early 1834 many of the old blue uniforms were still on hand and serviceable, although as of October 1832 Weed stopped requesting proposals for blue uniform coats (*DNI*, Oct. 27, 1832: 3.6). Thus, Jackson authorized the postponement of the issuance of new green uniforms until January 1, 1835, by which time it was hoped the supply of most of the old clothing would be exhausted.

Officers were to wear a grass-green coat with buff-white facings, and with two rows of ten buttons. The standing collar had two buff-white-edged

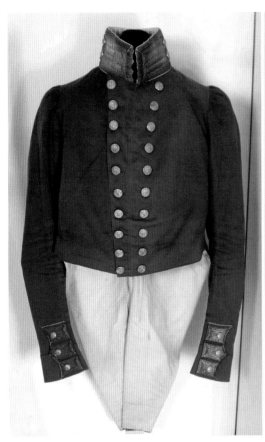
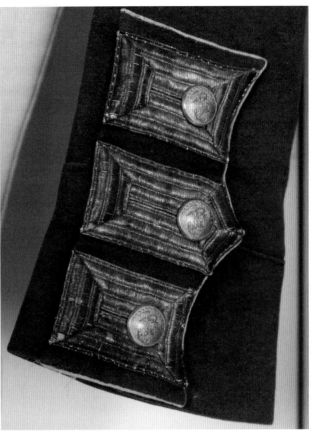

gold blind buttonholes either side, each terminating in a small button. Each sleeve had a 6½in-long slashed flap edged with buff on which were gold loops and small buttons – four for field officers, three for captains and staff officers, and two for lieutenants. Extending to the bend of the knee except for lieutenants, whose skirts were 3½in shorter, the skirts had slashed flaps with four buff-white-trimmed gold loops and large buttons, and buff-white "turnbacks." Two large buttons were attached at the rear waist. All buttons were gilt, convex, with eagle, anchor, and stars, and a raised border.

Officers' full-dress headgear consisted of a *chapeau*, and all wore an epaulet on each shoulder. That for field officers consisted of a plain gold cloth strap with brass crescent, and ½in-diameter gold, bright bullion fringe 3½in long. Epaulets for captains and staff officers, plus lieutenants, were the same except the fringe was narrower and only 2½in long. Staff officers were also distinguished by a gold aiguillette worn on the right shoulder under the epaulet. Trousers for all officers were of light gray with a 1½in-wide buff-white outer seam stripe for winter wear, and white linen drilling for summer.

Officers' full-dress rank insignia was further clarified on November 4, 1834, when gold epaulets with bullion fringe of different diameters according to rank were prescribed. As a colonel, Henderson wore epaulets with a silver embroidered eagle and wide bullion fringe. Lieutenant colonels had the same epaulet but without the eagle, and majors had the strap in silver but with a gold fringe, crescent, and edging to the strap.

Undress for officers consisted of a grass-green single-breasted frock coat, with plain collar and cuffs, fastened by ten large Marine Corps buttons, and

This Pattern 1834 grass-green double-breasted full-dress coat belonged to Levi Twiggs, who commanded the First Battalion of Marines during the Mexican–American War. Worn while he was a captain, this coat displays three gold loops and three small Marine Corps buttons on each cuff. Commissioned a second lieutenant in the Marine Corps on November 10, 1813, Twiggs saw action in the War of 1812 aboard the frigate USS *President*. Promoted to captain on February 23, 1830, Twiggs next saw action against the Seminoles in Florida during 1836–37. Promoted to major on November 15, 1840, he commanded the First Battalion of Marines in Mexico, and was killed during the assault on Chapultepec Castle on September 13, 1847. (National Museum of the Marine Corps: Accession No. 2008.3.4)

two smaller buttons of the same pattern securing each cuff. In January 1835, rank insignia for the undress coat was prescribed as shoulder straps with gold and silver leaves respectively for a lieutenant colonel and major, two bars for a captain, one for a first lieutenant, and none for a second lieutenant (MCA).

A 2in-wide white leather sword belt supported the Model 1826 Marine officer's sword, underneath which a sash of crimson silk net was worn. Footwear consisted of half boots worn under the trousers.

Full dress for sergeant majors and quartermaster sergeants consisted of the same double-breasted pattern coat as for officers with four loops of gold Prussia braid and buttons on the slashed sleeves, the same as was designated for field-grade officers. Skirts extended only to 3½in above the bend of the knee. Shoulder straps were plain buff-white cloth terminating in yellow cloth wings with worsted fringe in imitation of bullion. An aiguillette of yellow silk with gilt tags was attached under the epaulet strap on the left shoulder. A crimson net sash, with plain fringe, was worn under a white waist belt.

Sergeants wore a grass-green single-breasted coat fastened with nine large Marine Corps buttons. Shoulder straps, wings, and sleeve trim were the same as for sergeant majors. Shorter skirts extended to about 8in from the bend of the knee. Orderly sergeants wore a scarlet worsted waist sash. For winter wear, all sergeants wore a buff seam stripe on their light-gray trousers.

Corporals and privates wore the same uniform as sergeants, with the exception of having only two loops and buttons on the sleeves. Also their light-gray trousers were without seam stripes, and rank was determined by Army-pattern epaulets.

Headgear for all NCOs and other ranks consisted of a black leather bell-crown shako with leather visor, and brass scaled chinstrap, at the front of which was a 3in-wide brass "eagle," and a black leather cockade with an "anchor" button at center, above which was a 3½in-long yellow pompon with a brass ball at the bottom. On November 4, 1834, a "superior quality" bell-crown shako was prescribed for captains and lieutenants in place of a *chapeau* (RG 127, NARA). Footwear was straight-last shoes over which black cloth gaiters were worn under the trousers (RG 127, NARA).

Fatigue dress for enlisted Marines continued to be a gray jacket and trousers. By this time headgear consisted of a plain cloth fatigue cap with wide, stiffened top. When two recruits deserted from the Marine Rendezvous at Baltimore, MD, in April 1839, they were described as wearing "fatigue dress, grey round-jacket, grey pantaloons, and flat topped leather caps" (*TSB*, Apr. 22, 1839: 1.3).

Following the adoption of a linen jacket for warm weather wear, on February 17, 1834, Quartermaster Weed requested proposals for supplying 500 white "Linen Jackets" (*DG2*, Feb. 17, 1834: 3.5). On January 6, 1836, he required "2,500 Pair Linen Overalls, 1,000 Linen Jackets, 1,000 Pair of Gaiters … 800 Fatigue Caps" (*AS*, Jan. 8, 1836: 3.2). Further requests for these garments continued until the mid-1850s.

Accouterments for Model 1816 flintlock muskets continued to include whitened buff leather shoulder belts with a plain oval brass breast plate, a white waist belt fastened with a plain rectangular plate, and an Army-pattern cartridge box. As Marines usually only served aboard ship or ashore at ports, the field equipment issued was usually limited to a knapsack. Of box-pattern, this was covered with Russia sheeting, or hemp linen, painted black with white painted letters "USM" at its center. For extended field

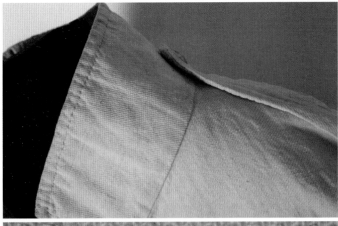

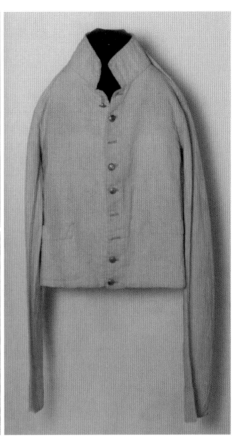

service during the Second Seminole War (1835–42), equipage such as musket slings, haversacks, and canteens were drawn from Army stores.

During the course of the remainder of the 1830s it was discovered that the green coats issued to the Marines quickly faded in the sun, especially at sea, and following numerous complaints, Major Augustus A. Nicholson, the Corps Quartermaster, advised Colonel Commandant Henderson on March 19, 1839:

> The 'green' is but illy adapted to service, but particularly so to Marine service, as the saline air is unfavourable to the durability of the colour, especially to that shade of green established for the uniform of the Marine-Corps. Manufacturers with whom I have consulted while at the head of the clothing-bureau at Philadelphia, have been of the opinion that it is rarely possible to have fast colours of that particular shade made, even for finer cloths, much less for that quality which is worn by the troops. (RG 80, NARA)

On May 29, 1839, President Martin Van Buren approved a change of uniform, and an order in July made the green uniform obsolete as of July 4, 1840. As the deadline for change approached, however, there was still a large supply of green dress coats in the possession of the Quartermaster. Accordingly, as was the case in 1834, a postponement was authorized on July 3, 1840, continuing the green dress uniform until further orders. These were finally issued on July 22, 1841, when the Marine Corps returned to navy-blue coats with scarlet facings and sky-blue or white trousers.

Also worn by Levi Twiggs, this US Army-pattern white linen fatigue jacket was sent back from Mexico after his death, and he likely intended it for off-duty wear once he had changed the buttons to Marine Corps pattern. Note the two pockets at the waist and the shoulder strap buttoned to the collar. (National Museum of the Marine Corps: Accession No. 1974.3611.1)

THE SECOND SEMINOLE WAR

The Indian policy of President Jackson provided the Marines with the next opportunity for large-scale active service. The cause of the conflict that flared up in Florida was the US Government's policy of resettling Native Americans west of the Mississippi River in order to open up their land to white settlers, and to re-capture numerous Black runaway slaves who had joined the ranks of the Seminole tribes. Although some of the Seminoles capitulated without much resistance, others refused to move and on December 28, 1835, attacked and massacred a column of Army troops under Brevet Major Francis L. Dade as it marched to the relief of Fort King. By April 1836 further trouble had developed as war broke out along the Chattahoochee River between the Creeks and the white settlers of Georgia and Alabama. With Army resources stretched to the limit, the War Department required more troops, and for the first time the Marines were detached for service with the Army under the provisions of the Act of June 30, 1834, by order of President Jackson.

For immediate service in Florida, a detachment of 57 Marines from USS *Constellation*, of Quasi-War fame, and the sloop-of-war USS *St. Louis*, both of the West India Squadron, arrived at St. Marks aboard the steamer *Eclipse* on January 15, 1836, and were dispatched under First Lieutenant Nathaniel S. Waldron in the chartered merchant brig *Seaflower* bound for Tampa Bay four days later. There they landed a shore party in support of the Army garrison at Fort Brooke and crewed small boats conducting amphibious patrols (*AG*, Feb. 6, 1836: 2.2).

Having tendered the service of the Marines for duty with the Army in the field, Henderson received orders during May 1836 to gather all the disposable force on shore, except for a sergeant's guard at each post, and to proceed south to report to Major General Winfield Scott, who had been given command of operations in Georgia, Alabama, and Florida on January 21, 1836. Arriving at Augusta, Georgia, on June 7, the First Battalion under Henderson, consisting of five companies composed of 21 officers and 254 men, marched overland 224 miles to Columbus, Georgia, where they established "Camp Henderson" 15 miles south of that city on the west bank of the Chattahoochee River. On July 1, 1836, they were joined by the Second Battalion, commanded by Brevet Lieutenant Colonel William H. Freeman and consisting of 14 officers and 143 men in three companies. Thus when

E · MARINES AT FORT BROOKE, 1836

Stationed at Fort Brooke, Florida, in 1836, the Marine captain (**1**) wears Pattern 1833 summer full dress including an officers' "superior quality" bell-crown shako with yellow worsted pompon, grass-green double-breasted coat with gold and buff trimming, and white linen fly-front trousers. Rank is indicated by epaulets on each shoulder consisting of a plain gold lace strap with brass crescent, a ¼in-diameter gold, bright bullion fringe, and three buff-edged gold loops on each cuff. His Model 1826 Marine officer's sword with "Mameluke" hilt is attached to a whitened buff leather waist belt which is fastened with a Pattern 1830 Navy officers' belt plate over a crimson silk net sash. He is examining a Seminole/Creek bandolier bag.

The private (**2**) wears Pattern 1834 summer full dress. His bell-crown shako has a smaller Army-pattern eagle plate attached; his grass-green single-breasted coat has yellow facings trimmed with buff. Black cloth gaiters are worn over his laced leather boots. He is armed with a .69-caliber Model 1816 flintlock musket, and his equipment consists of whitened buff leather shoulder belts, with plain oval breast plate, supporting an Army Pattern 1828 black leather cartridge box, plus bayonet.

The musician (**3**) wears an enlisted men's pattern bell-crown shako and a scarlet coatee with white "turnbacks"; epaulets and loops on cuffs were yellow trimmed with buff. With a red-painted shell, his drum is based on the pattern supplied by William Ent, of Germantown, Pennsylvania, from 1834. A musicians' brass-hilted sword is carried in a frog attached to a whitened buff leather shoulder sling.

fully formed, Henderson's Marine regiment consisted of 35 officers and 397 men organized into eight companies. Company-sized units and detachments of Marines spent the summer of 1836 patrolling the Georgia/Alabama border on foot and by boat, and had minor skirmishes with the Creeks led by Jim Henry.

On October 3, 1836, Henderson received orders to march his Marines south into Florida Territory as part of the force commanded by Major General Thomas S. Jesup. Stationed at Fort Brooke, a battalion of Marines took part in a fight with the Seminoles in the Great Cypress Swamp on January 27, 1837, as part of the Second Brigade, Army of the South, led by Henderson; his command also consisted of Army regulars, Alabama volunteers, and friendly Creeks. Making contact with the Seminoles, the Marines were ordered in pursuit. Penetrating the swampland for about 500yd they arrived at the Hatchee-Lustee River, a deep stream about 25yd wide. Observing felled trees protruding from each side of the river forming a natural bridge, Henderson extended his troops along the river and ordered crossfire brought to bear on the opposite bank, following which Captain John Harris, and several volunteer officers, ran across the fallen tree trunks, urging the enlisted Marines and volunteers to follow them. According to Henderson's report, the Seminoles were pursued "as rapidly as the deep swamp and their mode of warfare admitted" (Sprague 1848: 175). After several more firefights that were joined by Army Regulars, Alabama volunteers, and friendly Creeks, the Seminoles disappeared into the swampland.

The Marines sustained two killed and four wounded at Hatchee-Lustee. For his involvement in this action, Harris was brevetted a major in 1843 for "gallantry and good conduct" (CC, Mar. 16, 1843: 2.2). In his battle report, Henderson stated, "The regular troops, both artillery and Marines, displayed great bravery, and the most untiring and determined perseverance. The Marines, however, I cannot refrain from mentioning in a particular manner. The killed and wounded show where they were, and render any further comment from me unnecessary" (quoted in Sprague 1848: 176).

Having led one of the few successful engagements of the Seminole campaign of 1836, and for his service in Georgia and Alabama, Henderson was brevetted brigadier general, and as such became the first general in the history of the US Marine Corps. As a result of the action at Hatchee-Lustee, many Seminole chiefs finally agreed to move their people to a reservation in preparation for being transported west. With the war seemingly over, Henderson returned to Washington on May 23, leaving Lieutenant Colonel Samuel Miller as senior Marine officer in Florida, with Captain William W. Dulany in command of a two-company battalion of Marines in the field. A week later, however, 700 Seminoles at Tampa awaiting transportation were rescued by Chief Osceola, and hostilities recommenced in Florida. Although fighting continued for another five years, by the summer of 1838 all Marines were detached from duty with the Army in Florida. However, a large detachment of them continued to serve with the Navy in the Florida Squadron, also known as the "Mosquito Fleet."

On December 2, 1839, Lieutenant John T. McLaughlin USN was given command of a large combined force manned by sailors and Marines that consisted of three schooners, the *Wave*, *Flirt*, and *Otsego*, and five 20-oared, single-mast gun barges, for close-in offshore patrol along the Florida Keys to intercept Cuban and Bahamian traders bringing arms and other supplies to the Seminoles. In addition he had charge of about 60 canoes of various sizes ranging from 10ft to 40ft in length, which were to be used to probe the interior. McLaughlin also acquired from Havana, Cuba, bloodhounds with Spanish handlers to track down the Seminoles (*EP*, Apr. 8, 1840: 2.2).

On January 1, 1841, a combined expedition led by Brevet Colonel William S. Harney, 2d Dragoons, and consisting of 20 dragoons, 70 soldiers of the 3d Artillery, and 90 sailors and 60 Marines under McLaughlin, set off to search the Everglades for the encampment of Abiaka, or Sam Jones, chief of the Miccosukee, a Seminole–Muscogee Creek tribe. With the exception of four or five large canoes carrying from six to ten men each, this force was distributed in small canoes specially made for the purpose and carrying five men each. Every man carried 20 days' rations and 60 rounds of ball ammunition. Silence was maintained by all, and orders were communicated by signal whistles supplied to each officer. When in motion, the canoes progressed in single file and open order, being 20 paces apart. Each man was ordered to "drop his paddle and seize his musket at a moment's notice" (*CC*, Mar. 23, 1841: 2.4).

Reaching the hammocks, or islands in the grass water, believed to be occupied by Sam Jones, on January 5, Harney found them deserted. Of this occasion, an anonymous member of expedition wrote, "Our greatest annoyance at this place, was the immense number of fleas, cockroaches and musquitoes [*sic*]; everything you touched, even the ground was alive with the former, which, with musquitoes, attacked us, while the roaches luxuriated on our provisions" (*CC*, Mar. 23, 1841: 2.2).

After finding and killing only three warriors, Harney decided to end his search for Sam Jones, while McLaughlin continued the expedition and, on January 12, led his sailors and Marines west across the Everglades in search of Spanish Seminoles who were believed to have gathered to the west. Although they encountered and killed only one Seminole during their week-long trek, they finally paddled out of the grass water and reached the Gulf Coast on January 19, 1841, being the first whites to cross the full breadth of the Everglades.

Uniform, arms, and equipment 1841–59

The 1839 Regulations, which were republished in 1852 by order of Brevet Brigadier General Commandant Henderson, were basically a change of coat color from grass green trimmed with buff-white to navy blue trimmed with scarlet, with the remaining uniform pattern and much of the rank insignia the same as that for 1834. Trousers for field officers, captains, and lieutenants were sky blue and staff wore dark blue. All trousers had a 1½in-wide dark-blue stripe edged with scarlet. Summer trousers were white linen drilling. All officers' winter trousers were changed to dark blue with 1¾in-wide scarlet stripes sewn along the outside seam.

Full-dress headgear for field officers, staff, and captains consisted of a *chapeau* with a cockade, gilt loop and button, tassel, and scarlet fountain plume. Other company-grade officers wore the bell-crown shako of blue cloth with black patent-leather visor and twilled silk band around the bottom and sides, surmounted by a scarlet feather plume. The cap plate for all ranks from 1839 through 1846 consisted of an eagle perched on a foul anchor, with an arc of 13 stars above, on a shield set within a wreath. In 1846 this was replaced with a simpler eagle-and-anchor plate. Officers could acquire their caps from the quartermaster department, but were required to have all metal parts on them gold plated. Bell-crown shakos for NCOs and privates

This Huddy and Duval lithograph shows a Marine private at "carry arms" in Pattern 1839 full dress complete with bell-crown shako adorned with a red pompon and eagle plate; dark-blue coat trimmed in red with yellow lace and epaulets; white belts and dress gloves; and light-blue trousers. The dark-blue seam stripes on the trousers are inaccurate, as privates were prescribed plain trousers for full and undress. (Courtesy of the Anne S.K. Brown Military Collection, RI)

Published in the *Regulations for the Uniform & Dress of the Navy and Marine Corps* in 1852, these plates show elements for full and undress Marine uniforms as prescribed in 1839. At center in the upper illustration is the uniform dress *chapeau* worn by field officers, staff, and captains, and undress shoulder straps for colonels, lieutenant colonels, majors, captains, and first lieutenants. Either side of this are examples of the number of loops indicating rank on collar, cuffs, and coat tails, plus examples of large and small buttons. The lower illustration shows a lieutenant's bell-crown shako with plate, and officers' undress cap with insignia consisting of a foul anchor in wreath. The "Mameluke"-pattern hilt of a Model 1826 Marine officer's sword in frog is at center, with the design of the officer's sword clasp at bottom right. (Internet Archive)

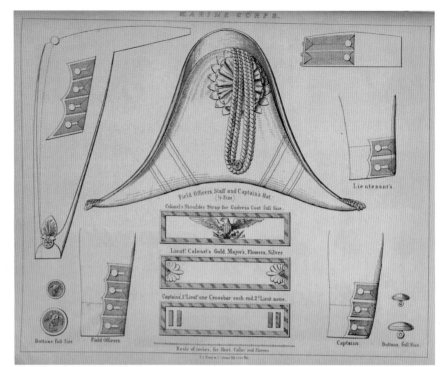

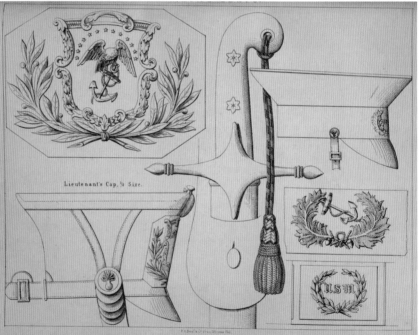

were surmounted with a 3½in-long scarlet pompon, which was replaced in 1845 by a round pompon with ⅓ red top and ⅔ dark-blue bottom on a long stem. This change was not included in the 1852 Regulations, however, either because of an oversight or because it was deemed unimportant as everyone concerned knew what was being provided and worn.

Undress for field-grade officers, staff, and captains, consisted of a navy-blue double-breasted frock coat with roll collar. This had two rows

of ten large "eagle, anchor and star" buttons, three small buttons of the same pattern on cuffs, and three large buttons in the rear folds of the tails. Lieutenants wore a single-breasted ten-button coat. Rank was designated by a blue cloth shoulder strap, 4in long and 1in wide, with gold embroidered edge ⅛in wide, on each shoulder. That of colonel bore a gold spread eagle; lieutenant colonel a gold embroidered flower at each end of the shoulder strap; major the same in silver; captain two gold bars; first lieutenant one bar; second lieutenant plain strap.

A navy-blue cloth or kerseymere shell jacket was also permitted for officers' winter undress, edged with gold lace, and fastened with one row of 16 small Marine buttons on the left breast and an equivalent number of hooks on the right breast, plus three yellow gilt hooks and eyes on the collar and the same fastening the cuffs. Summer wear consisted of a plain white linen shell jacket with hooks and eyes throughout.

Winter undress trousers for all officers were dark blue without stripes. Fatigue caps for officers were dark-blue cloth with a black patent-leather visor and ¾in-wide chinstrap, with insignia consisting of a foul anchor set within a wreath. Footwear for officers consisted of ankle or Jefferson boots.

Full dress for NCOs and privates was also based on the 1834 pattern, with navy blue and scarlet trim replacing grass green and buff. The ranks of sergeant major and quartermaster sergeant were indicated by a bullion fringe on epaulets, and an aiguillette of yellow silk with gilt tags worn on the left shoulder. Corporals wore yellow worsted epaulets with worsted fringe in imitation of bullion, while privates' shoulder knots were without a fringe. In 1851, the latter were replaced by brass counter-straps or shoulder scales (*DR*, Aug. 15, 1851: 3.2).

Worn by Levi Twiggs as a major, this Pattern 1839 navy-blue uniform dress coat has four red-trimmed gold loops on each cuff commensurate with his rank. A small embroidered gold "shell and flame" was sewn at the bottom of each skirt tail. (National Museum of the Marine Corps: Accession No. 2008.3.1)

All NCOs above the rank of corporal, whether in full or undress, were distinguished by 1½in-wide dark-blue stripes edged with scarlet on their sky-blue trousers. Those trousers worn by all other ranks were plain sky blue. Musicians continued to wear scarlet coats trimmed with white.

Fatigue dress for enlisted men changed from a light-gray to a sky-blue shell jacket with plain collar, shoulder straps, and cuffs. A notice published in August 1841 described a deserter as wearing "a light blue cloth jacket, pantaloons the same, and flat topped leather cap" (*TS*, Aug. 31, 1841: 1.3). A "fatigue frock" of unknown pattern was also part of a clothing request on September 17, 1857 (*ES*, Sep. 28, 1857: 4.5).

Fatigue-dress headgear consisted of a navy-blue cap with the brass letters "USM" at front (*DR*, Aug. 15, 1851: 3.2). Summer wear consisted of a plain white linen jacket and trousers. Rank insignia for sergeants when in fatigue dress consisted of two plain stripes of worsted lace on each arm below the elbow, placed diagonally on the upper side of the arm from one seam to the other, the outer points inclining toward the elbow. Corporals wore one stripe of the same pattern. By the mid-1840s footwear for enlisted men consisted of left- and right-foot brogans.

The Marine Corps began to receive the .69-caliber Model 1835 flintlock musket just before the Mexican–American War (1846–48). Permission was received from the Ordnance Department to send the first of these to the Watertown Arsenal in Massachusetts for conversion to percussion on November 4, 1852. During October 1853, Marine Corps detachments began to receive .69-caliber Model 1842 percussion smoothbore muskets. In April 1857 some .69-caliber Remington/Maynard-conversion Model 1816 rifled muskets with tape primers were received, although the Marines preferred to use the percussion cap for better results (McAuley 1999: 42). Equipage continued to be whitened buff leather waist belts. Pattern 1857 black leather

cartridge boxes had a plain outer flap without an oval plate. Pattern 1850 cap pouches in black leather were also carried.

In line with its previous field service during the Second Seminole War, the Marine regiment involved in the Mexican–American War drew much of its equipment and some of its clothing from the Army. During November/December 1847, Second Lieutenant Daniel J. Sutherland received headgear, clothing, and equipment for Co. A of the Marine Battalion from the Army Quartermaster's Stores: this included forage caps, jackets, wool and flannel shirts, bootees, overalls, and stocks, plus knapsacks, canteens, and haversacks (Milligan 2005: 42).

THE MEXICAN–AMERICAN WAR

War between Mexico and the United States was the inevitable result of the westward expansion that had been taking place since 1814. Some of the first Americans to set foot on Mexican soil after the battle of Resaca de la Palma on May 9, 1846, were Marines of the frigates USS *Cumberland* and USS *Potomac* in a naval force of about 200 under Captain John H. Aulick USN that assisted the Army in occupying La Burrita, some 15 miles north of the mouth of the Rio Grande River. Throughout the remainder of the Mexican–American War, the Marine Corps played an important role on the Pacific and Gulf Mexican coasts with forces that landed at places such as Tampico, San Juan Bautista, Yerba Buena, and Los Angeles.

On July 7, 1846, 85 Marines were among the 250-strong naval force under Commodore John D. Sloat that landed at Monterey to annex California for the United States and hoist the "Stars and Stripes" flag over the customs

Worn by Major Levi Twiggs, this navy-blue coat was authorized as an inexpensive day dress wear for officers, who could choose whatever style they preferred as long as it had two rows of ten buttons, and either epaulets or shoulder straps. The buttons are of "eagle, anchor and star" pattern, with three small buttons of the same pattern on the cuffs, two on the rear waist, and three in the rear folds of the tails. Rank is further indicated by the rolling collar and a silver embroidered flower at each end of the shoulder straps. The left sleeve lining has been marked, "FROM / CHAS C. WATSON & SONS / 92 CHESTNUT ST / PHILADA," and is signed "Majr L. Twiggs." (National Museum of the Marine Corps: Accession No. 2008.3.5)

house on Calle Principal. During October 1846, Marines formed part of a force of about 285 men under Captain William Mervine USN that mounted an unsuccessful attempt to re-take Los Angeles following a revolt among Californians led by José María Flores, Governor and Comandante General *pro tem* of Alta California during 1846–47. After further actions involving Marine detachments, Los Angeles and most of Upper California was brought under permanent control with the signing of the Treaty of Cahuenga on January 13, 1847. Other Marine involvement in landings and actions at San Diego, La Paz, Loreto, Guaymas, and San Jose secured Lower California and the west coast of Mexico by April 1848.

With most of the volunteers in the Army involved in the war in Mexico due to be discharged having signed up for only a year, Congress authorized an increase in the Regular Army and Marine Corps in March 1847. The Marines were increased by 12 officers, 30 each of sergeants, corporals, drummers, and fifers, plus 1,000 enlisted men. This enlarged the Marine Corps from 42 officers and 986 men to 54 officers and 2,106 men. Many of the new recruits served in battalion-sized units rather than as a full regiment due to reluctance on the part of Commodore Matthew C. Perry to relinquish control of his Marines serving along the Gulf Coast, a detachment of which served alongside the Army's 3d Artillery during the campaign to capture Veracruz.

Commanded by Brevet Lieutenant Colonel Samuel E. Watson, the Marines assigned to Mexico consisted of six companies organized into two battalions with Major Levi Twiggs leading the First Battalion, composed of companies A, B, and C, and Brevet Major William W. Dulany the Second Battalion, consisting of companies D, E, and F. Containing only 314 officers and men, these units were redesignated as a single Marine Battalion by June 1847. As part of Brevet Major General Persifor F. Smith's brigade, Major General John A. Quitman's division, the Battalion took part in the assault on Chapultepec Castle (later misnamed "the Halls of Montezuma") in Mexico City on September 13, 1847. Twiggs spearheaded the attack of the volunteer division with a party of 120 Marines and soldiers while Captain John G. Reynolds, a company commander and one of the ablest officers in

Marines spearheaded the attack on Chapultepec Castle on September 13, 1847. As part of Brevet Major General Persifor F. Smith's 1st Brigade, 2d Division, they advanced up to the castle on the Tacubaya causeway visible in the foreground of this lithograph by Nathaniel Currier. (Library of Congress LC-DIG-pga-02604)

the Marine Corps, followed with a group of pioneers carrying scaling ladders and pickaxes. The remaining Marines under Watson acted in support.

As the surrounding terrain was extremely swampy, the US forces had to stay on the Tacubaya causeway with a deep ditch either side in order to approach Chapultepec Castle and Mexico City. Reaching a point about 200yd from the gate of the castle, Twiggs' storming party was forced to take cover in the ditch to return fire. At the same time, Watson's troops and several other storming parties sought refuge in the same ditch. Attempting to rally his men and lead them on, Twiggs was shot dead by musketry fire from the castle. Elsewhere, a detachment of Marines from Co. C under Captain George H. Terrett advanced ahead of the rest of Watson's command and overran an enemy battery.

Following the capture of Chapultepec Castle, elements of Smith's brigade pressed on along the causeway to the Garita de Belén at Mexico City. Once his troops reached that point, Quitman ordered the enemy breastwork lowered so that one of the captured guns could be turned and brought to bear on the remaining Mexican artillerists who were showering the Americans with grapeshot. Quick to respond, Dulany and two junior Marine officers successfully tore down parts of the enemy breastwork, thereby enabling a gun to be trained low enough to return fire. A report of the incident published in the *Philadelphia Inquirer* stated that "the Major and his men were kept

F **TO THE HALLS OF MONTEZUMA, 1847**

Scrambling up toward the gate of the Military College of Chapultepec the Marine captain (**1**) shouts orders. He wears undress composed of a Pattern 1839 fatigue cap with foul-anchor-within-wreath insignia. Rank insignia on his double-breasted frock coat are blue cloth shoulder straps with two silver bars at each end of the strap. His sky-blue, fly-front trousers have dark-blue seam stripes edged with scarlet, side pockets, and white bone buttons. He carries a Model 1826 Marine officer's sword with "Mameluke" hilt in a brass scabbard attached to a black patent-leather waist belt, fastened by a Pattern 1839 plate with gold Old English letters "USM" within a silver wreath.

The private (**2**) wears a Pattern 1839 fatigue cap with brass letters "USM" at front, and fatigue dress consisting of a sky-blue shell jacket with plain collar and cuffs; and plain sky-blue, fly-front trousers. He is armed with a .69-caliber Model 1835 flintlock musket.

Also wearing fatigue dress and cap, the musician (**3**) is armed with a sword with solid brass hilt and carried in a frog attached to a whitened buff leather shoulder sling. His drum is of the type made by William H. Horstmann & Sons, of Philadelphia. Both the private and musician are equipped with haversack and small metal canteen.

These uniform trousers were worn by Major Levi Twiggs. Of sky-blue kersey, they have 1½in-wide dark-blue seam stripes edged with scarlet. They have six brass buttons on the fly and a larger brass button closure at the waist. Brass suspender buttons are sewn around the exterior waistband, which is pointed at the center rear. There is one waist pocket on the right side. The interior waistband has the inscription "L Twiggs." (National Museum of the Marine Corps: Accession No. 2008.3.2)

at work for some time, every shot making sad havoc among the men, horses and mules engaged in this perilous duty" (*PI*, Apr. 3, 1848: 2.3).

Indicative of the bravery of the Marines at Chapultepec Castle, 13 of the 23 Marine officers present received brevets. Among the officers was the Commandant's son, Second Lieutenant Charles A. Henderson, who commanded another pioneer storming party, and First Lieutenant John S. Devlin, who served as Acting Assistant Quartermaster.

Later that day, the Marines were among the first American troops to fight their way into Mexico City. After the Mexican surrender, they were given the task of clearing the Palacio Nacional of plunderers and vagabonds while, atop the building, Second Lieutenant Augustus S. Nicholson, who later became the Adjutant and Inspector General of the Marine Corps, cut down the Mexican tricolor and ordered a Marine sergeant to run up the "Stars and Stripes" flag. The Marines sustained a total of 11 killed and 28 wounded during the war with Mexico (Bauer 1975: 398).

After the conflict, the Marine Corps was presented with its first stand of colors, which bore the motto "From Tripoli to the Halls of the Montezumas" inspired by its earlier success at Derna in 1805 and recent subjugation of Mexico (*DET* Mar. 18, 1848: 4.1). Later in the 1880s, these lines were adapted to a march tune taken from Jacques Offenbach's comic opera *Geneviève de Brabant*, and eventually became known as the "Marine Hymn," which today is recognized as one of the foremost US service songs.

EXPANDING EMPIRE

In the years following the Mexican–American War, a three-fold increase in American foreign trade further expanded the horizons of both the Navy and Marine Corps. On the coast of South America, Marines were landed at Buenos Aires, Argentina, in 1852 to protect American lives and property during fighting between the ruling classes of Buenos Aires and the Argentine Provinces.

On March 11, 1853, a detachment of Marines off the sloop-of-war USS *Cyane*, commanded by Orderly Sergeant James Thompson, was landed to protect the interests of Cornelius Vanderbilt's Accessory Transit Company in and near Greytown, or San Juan del Norte, Nicaragua. Conveying gold from California to the United States since 1850, the operation of this company was being disrupted by the local inhabitants who had recently been given independence from indirect British control. After several days' guard duty, and with the ominous guns of *Cyane* supporting their presence, matters were temporarily calmed and the Marines were withdrawn two days later.

Matters came to a head again in Greytown on May 16, 1853, when Solon Borland, the American Envoy Extraordinary and Minister Plenipotentiary (Nicaragua), was mobbed and besieged in the house of an American commercial agent. With the United States demanding the punishment of those responsible, the *Cyane* returned to the harbor and Commander George H. Hollins allowed 24 hours for the population to evacuate before he commenced shelling Greytown, reducing much of it to rubble, following which a landing party of Marines and sailors completed its destruction. In December 1857, the Marines again went ashore in Nicaragua at Puntas Arenas, across the harbor from Greytown, to arrest the revolutionary and

filibuster William Walker, and 132 of his followers, who had established an encampment there in an attempt to create a slave-owning republic (Nalty 1968: 2–3).

A battalion of 200 Marines commanded by Major Jacob Zeilin accompanied Commodore Matthew C. Perry on his historic expedition across the Pacific Ocean to open diplomatic and trade relations with Japan in 1853. Unsure what reception to expect on landing at Yedo (present-day Tokyo), Perry sent Zeilin's battalion ashore with orders to either parade or fight. Responding to a peaceful welcome, Perry's column of officers and enlisted seamen progressed to the ceremonial pavilion to exchange gifts with the Japanese.

On April 4, 1854, 70 Marines and sailors off the American sloop-of-war USS *Plymouth* and 150 Royal Marines and sailors from the British screw sloop HMS *Encounter* landed at Shanghai, one of the five treaty ports imposed on China by the Western powers for international trade, to protect

Part of a silk-bound scroll by an anonymous Japanese artist, this painting shows Marines drilling during Commodore Matthew C. Perry's historic expedition across the Pacific Ocean to open diplomatic and trade relations with Japan in 1853. Marine musicians in full dress are at center right. The Marines in formation shown wearing epaulets are the detachment's sergeants and corporals. (Courtesy of the Anne S.K. Brown Military Collection, RI)

Published by George W. Hatch and Charles Severyn, of 140 Fulton Street, New York, this lithograph depicts the American expedition, under Commodore Matthew C. Perry, landing in Japan on July 14, 1853. The Marines under Major Jacob Zeilin are formed at right. (Library of Congress LC-DIG-pga-08972)

several English residents who had been attacked by Chinese Imperialist troops during the Taiping Rebellion. In the ensuing assault on their fortified encampment, the Chinese fired on the advancing Americans with their *jingals*, or swivel guns, killing one Marine and wounding several sailors, before being overrun and driven off (*PD*, Jun. 28, 1854: 2.2).

On August 4, 1855, 26 Marines led by First Lieutenant James H. Jones from the sidewheel steam frigate USS *Powhatan*, under Commodore William J. McCluney, commander of the US Navy's East Indies Squadron, took part in a combined American–British operation against a fleet of 14 large Chinese piratical junks mounting 16–18 guns, and 22 smaller ones, along with seven captured merchant ships. Two days earlier the British steam screw sloop HMS *Rattler*, commanded by Commodore William A. Fellowes, had chased the Chinese vessels into the shallow waters of Ty-Ho Bay where they dropped anchor. Reinforced by *Powhatan*, the launches and boats of both *Powhatan* and *Rattler*, each armed with a Dahlgren boat howitzer, went in to attack. The Marines from *Powhatan* were commanded by future Confederate Navy officer Lieutenant Robert B. Pegram.

The Chinese pirates began a heavy fire, but most of their round shot and grapeshot was not well directed and passed overhead. When in range the boats of *Powhatan* and *Rattler* started their return fire and sank six of the junks. As the range decreased to close quarters, each boat's crew singled out a remaining junk and boarded it, engaging in furious hand-to-hand fighting. Among the American casualties sustained were four Marines who were seriously wounded, including Private Benjamin F. Adamson who was among "the first to gain the enemy's deck" and greatly distinguished himself before being mortally wounded in the groin (*CG*, Nov. 2, 1855: 3.1). As result of the action, approximately 500 Chinese pirates were killed, wounded, or drowned, and around 1,000 were taken prisoner; 20 junks were destroyed and 16 smaller vessels escaped.

As a result of vessels of the East Indies Squadron, under Commodore James Armstrong, observing British operations against Chinese Imperialists in the treaty port of Canton during November 1856, Marines became involved in some of the fiercest fighting since the Mexican–American War. On November 15, guns from the "Barrier Forts" fired on a pinnace carrying future Union Navy admiral Commander Andrew H. Foote, commander of the sloop-

---

G   MARINES IN JAPAN, 1853

Accompanying Commodore Matthew C. Perry's historic expedition across the Pacific Ocean to open diplomatic and trade relations with Japan in 1853, a Marine captain and two corporals in 1839 Regulations summer uniform dress perform ceremonial duty ashore in Japan.

The captain (**1**) wears a *chapeau* with a cockade, gilt loop and button, tassel, and feather plume. His double-breasted tail-coat has two gold and buff-trimmed blind buttonholes either side of its scarlet-edged standing collar, each terminating in a small button. His sleeves have slashed flaps edged with scarlet, on which are three scarlet-trimmed gold loops, and small buttons. Epaulets with a plain gold strap, brass crescent, and gold, bright bullion fringe are worn on both shoulders. Trousers are plain white linen with fly front. His Model 1826 Marine officer's sword with "Mameluke" hilt in a brass scabbard is attached to a whitened buff leather waist belt with an 1839 Regulations plate bearing Gothic letters "USM" in silver wreath, under which is a crimson silk net sash.

The first corporal (**2**) wears an enlisted men's pattern bell-crown shako with scarlet pompon; and a scarlet-trimmed single-breasted tail-coat with two loops and buttons on each side of the collar and on each cuff. Rank is indicated by a yellow worsted epaulet with narrow worsted fringe on each shoulder. His white cotton trousers have a fly front. He is armed with a .69-caliber Model 1835 percussion musket. Accouterments consist of a Pattern 1829 black leather cartridge box with plain flap, and cap pouch; a whitened buff leather shoulder sling; a bayonet sling of the same material with a plain oval brass plate; and a white waist belt with a small plain rectangular brass plate.

The other corporal (**3**) is armed and uniformed in the same manner; privates lacked the epaulet fringes. He carries a canvas-covered, box-pattern knapsack, with brown leather straps, painted black with white letters "USM" within an oval border.

Entitled "The Attack on the Barrier Forts near Canton, China," this lithograph by John H. Bufford shows the shallow-draught steamer *Cum Fa* towing boats carrying the storming party of Marines and sailors toward the shore in the Pearl River during the action on November 20, 1856. Meanwhile, the guns of the sloops-of-war USS *Portsmouth* and USS *Levant* provide covering fire. (Naval History and Heritage Command NH 56895)

of-war USS *Portsmouth*, who was on his way to Canton to order the sailors and Marines guarding the American trade "factory" to evacuate their post to maintain US neutrality during the Chinese imperialists' fight with the British. Although there were no casualties, Armstrong considered this an insult to the "Stars and Stripes" flag and demanded within 24 hours an apology from Yeh Ming-Ch'en, Chinese viceroy and imperial commissioner, but the latter was unapologetic and demanded the US Navy warships withdraw from the forts.

In readiness for the assault on November 20, launches and cutters were manned with a storming party towed by the shallow-draught steamer *Cum Fa*, with Napier's Fort at the entrance to Fiddler's Reach chosen for the attack. To prepare the way, a launch from the screw frigate USS *San Jacinto* was sent ahead to take soundings which were successfully completed despite the "leadsman," Landsman John Mullins, being decapitated by a Chinese shell fired during the first attempt to check the depth of water.

Despite shot whistling and roaring around the boats as they approached the shore, the storming party, carrying a hastily prepared flag bearing the motto "Remember Mullins," and consisting of 200 sailors spearheaded by about 50 Marines commanded by Brevet Captain John D. Sims, Jr., lost only three killed and three wounded due to the inability of the Chinese to depress their guns to point-blank range. Within 10 minutes the sailors and Marines had crossed a deep ditch and were inside Napier's Fort, which the Chinese had abandoned. After spiking the fort's guns and burning or destroying what they could, the storming party went on during the next few days to capture the three remaining forts, while the boats followed them along the shoreline. As they approached the last fort to be captured, the Chinese mounted a counterattack using "rockets and arrows," which was easily beaten off by the Marines, plus a howitzer from *Portsmouth* (*DG*, Jan. 26, 1857: 4.2). As a result, about 250 Chinese defenders were killed or wounded at a loss of seven American dead and 22 wounded.

HARPERS FERRY

On the night of Sunday, October 16, 1859, the abolitionist John Brown and his small "army" of 22 men captured the United States Arsenal at Harpers Ferry, Virginia, in a vain attempt to incite an armed slave rebellion throughout the South. Quickly surrounded by local militia, Brown and his followers took hostages including Colonel Lewis W. Washington, great-grandnephew of George Washington, and fortified themselves in a brick-built engine house. Shortly after noon the next day, Colonel John Harris, who had been appointed Commandant of the Marine Corps on January 7, 1859, received an order from Secretary of the Navy Isaac Toucey to send "all the available Marines at Head Quarters … by this evening's train of cars to Harpers Ferry to protect the public property at that place, which is endangered by a riotous outbreak" (MCA).

Within several hours, First Lieutenant Israel Greene had 86 Marines plus two 12-pounder Dahlgren howitzers westbound on the Baltimore and Ohio Railroad headed for the scene of the insurrection; 150 soldiers from Fort Monroe, Virginia, also received orders to follow. All were to be commanded by Lieutenant Colonel Robert E. Lee of the 2d US Cavalry, who was on leave from frontier duty in Texas. The Marines disembarked about 1 mile short of Harpers Ferry at 2200hrs that night, where they were joined by Lee and First

This hand-colored engraving entitled "The storming of the engine-house by the United States Marines," was originally published in *Frank Leslie's Illustrated Newspaper* on October 29, 1859, and depicts the closing stages of the siege of Harpers Ferry, with Marines battering the doors down with a heavy ladder. Private Luke Quinn, the only Marine killed during the assault, is shown being attended to in the foreground. (GRANGER – Historical Photo Archive/Alamy Stock Photo)

Lieutenant J.E.B. Stuart, 1st US Cavalry, who served as his aide. The Marines were marched across the railroad bridge, and by midnight had occupied the Arsenal grounds where they surrounded the engine house.

Waiting until dawn on October 18, Lee held a council of war with his fellow officers. With hostages being held by Brown, it was impossible to use the howitzers. Hence Lee decided to send Stuart under a flag of truce at sunrise to attempt to persuade Brown to surrender. If this failed, Stuart was to raise his arm as a "signal," and the Marines would rush the doors of the engine house. Predictably, Brown would not accept Lee's terms, and an assault by 24 Marines led by Greene began immediately. A newspaper correspondent present wrote:

> Immediately the signal for attack was given, and the marines ... advanced in two lines on each side of the door. Two powerful fellows sprang between the lines, and with heavy sledge hammers attempted to batter down the door. The door swung and swayed, but appeared to be secured with a rope ... Failing thus to obtain a breach, the marines were ordered to fall back, and twenty of them took hold of a ladder, some forty feet long, and advancing at a run, brought it with tremendous power against the door. At the second blow it gave way, one leaf falling inward in a slanting position. The marines immediately advanced to the breach, Major [William W.] Russell [the Marine Corps Paymaster who, as a staff officer, could not command] and Lieutenant Greene leading the way. A marine in the front fell; the firing from the interior is rapid and sharp, they fire with deliberate aim, and for the moment the resistance is serious and desperate enough to excite the spectators to something like a pitch of frenzy. The next moment the marines pour in, the firing ceases, and the work was done, whilst the cheers rang from every side, the general feeling being that the marines had done their part admirably. (DD, Oct. 20, 1859: 1.4)

During the melée, Brown was wounded by a blow from Greene's dress sword, while all but two of his followers were either killed or captured. Two Marines were wounded and Irish-born Private Luke Quinn was killed. A further 148 Marines would give their lives, and 131 would be wounded, during the American Civil War that ensued from 1861 through 1865 to preserve the Union and abolish slavery in the United States.

H **MARINES AT HARPERS FERRY, 1859**

In the aftermath of the action on October 18, 1859, a Marine first lieutenant shows the men a pike intended for use during the slave rebellion John Brown hoped would start following his raid on the Arsenal at Harpers Ferry, Virginia.

The sergeant in fatigue dress (**1**) wears a Pattern 1839 fatigue cap with brass letters "USM" at front; a black leather stock; a plain sky-blue shell jacket with rank indicated by three yellow Army-pattern chevrons with points up on each arm below the elbow; and sky-blue fly-front trousers with a 1½in-wide dark-blue seam stripe edged with scarlet. He is armed with a .69-caliber Model 1842 Springfield rifled musket. Accouterments consist of whitened buff leather shoulder slings, with a plain oval brass plate, supporting a black leather cartridge box with plain flap, and a double frog holding a bayonet and an NCO sword. A cap pouch is carried on his buff leather waist belt, which has a plain brass plate.

Also in fatigue dress and armed and accoutered in the same manner, minus NCO sword, the private (**2**) wears a sky-blue single-breasted watch coat, and plain sky-blue trousers.

The first lieutenant (**3**) wears a Pattern 1839 officers' fatigue cap with a gold embroidered wreath and anchor. Rank is shown on his plain double-breasted undress frock coat by dark-blue shoulder straps with one gold bar at each end. His trousers are plain dark blue. He carries a Model 1826 Marine officer's sword with "Mameluke" hilt attached to a black patent-leather waist belt, fastened by a rectangular plate with silver Old English letters "USM" within a gold wreath.

SELECT BIBLIOGRAPHY

Adams, Charles Francis (1851). *The Works of John Adams*, Vol. 3, Boston, MA: Charles C. Little and James Brown.

Anonymous (1852). *Regulations for the Uniform and Dress of the Navy and Marine Corps of the United States*. Philadelphia, PA: Printed for the Navy Department by T.K. & P.G. Collins.

Bauer, K. Jack (1975). *The Mexican War 1846–1848*. New York, NY: Macmillan Publishing Co., Inc.

Clark, William Bell, ed. (1966). *Naval Documents of the American Revolution*, Vol. 2. Washington, DC: US Government Printing Office.

Clark, William Bell, ed. (1969). *Naval Documents of the American Revolution*, Vol. 4. Washington, DC: US Government Printing Office.

Clowes, W. Laird (1897). *The Royal Navy: A History from the Earliest Times to the Present*, Vol. VI. London: S. Low, Marston & Co.

Collum, Capt. Richard S., USMC (1891). "Extracts from the Journal of William Jennison, Jr., Lieutenant of Marines in the Continental Navy," *The Pennsylvania Magazine of History and Biography* 15.1: 101–08.

Cureton, Dr. Charles H. (2006). "Early Marine Corps Swords," *American Society of Arms Collectors Bulletin* 93: 93–133.

Cureton, Lt. Col. Charles H., & David M. Sullivan (2009). *The Civil War Uniforms of the United States Marine Corps: The Regulations of 1859*. San Jose, CA: R. James Bender Publications.

Debates and Proceedings in the Congress of the United States (1798). Fifth Congress, May 15, 1797, to March 3, 1790. Washington, DC: Gales & Seaton.

de Koven, Mrs. Reginald (1913). *The Life and Letters of John Paul Jones*, Vol. 1. New York, NY: Charles Scribner's Sons.

Field, Edward (1898). *Esek Hopkins, Commander-in-Chief of the Continental Navy during the American Revolution 1775 to 1778*. Providence, RI: The Preston & Rounds Co.

"General Records of the Department of the Navy," RG 80, National Archives & Records Administration.

Griffin, Martin I.J. (1903). *Commodore John Barry*. Philadelphia, PA: published by the author.

Jackson, I.R. (1840). *The Life of William Henry Harrison*. Philadelphia, PA: W. Marshall & Co.

Journal of the Continental Congress, Vol. 3. Washington Government Printing Office, 1905.

"Letters from the Commandant and other officers of the Marine Corps, January 1828–December 1886," RG 80, General Records of the Department of the Navy, 1804–1944; National Archives & Records Administration.

McAuley, John D. (1999). *Civil War Small Arms of the U.S. Navy and Marine Corps*. Lincoln, RI: Andrew Mowbray Publishers.

McClellan, Maj. Edwin N. (1925–1931). *History of the United States Marine Corps*, Vols. 1–3. Quantico, VA: Historical Section, US Marine Corps.

MCA = Marine Corps Archives, Alfred M. Gray Research Center, Quantico, VA.

Milligan, Lt. Col. Edward S. (2005). "Marine Corps Issues from U.S. Army Quartermaster Stores, Mexico City, 1847–1848," *Military Collector & Historian* 57.1: 42.

Nalty, Bernard C. (1968). *The United States Marines in Nicaragua*. Washington, DC: Historical Branch, G-3 Division, HQ, US Marine Corps.

NRC = "Naval Records Collection of the Office of Naval Records and Library," RG 45, National Archives & Records Administration.

Prentiss, Charles, compiler (1813). *The Life of the Late Gen. William Eaton*. Brookfield, MA: E. Merriam & Co.

PWD = "Papers of the War Department, 1784–1800," Roy Rosenzweig Center for History and New Media, or Letters Sent by the Secretary of Navy to Officers, March 1798–September 1886. M149, RG 45, National Archives & Records Administration.

"Records of the U.S. Marine Corps," RG 127, National Archives & Records Administration.

Sherburne, John Henry (1825). *Life and Character of the Chevalier John Paul Jones*. Washington, DC: Vanderpool & Cole.

Sprague, John T. (1848). *The origin, progress, and conclusion of the Florida war*. New York, NY: D. Appleton & Co.

Taylor, Bayard (1860). *A Visit to India, China, and Japan*. New York, NY: G.P. Putnam, 115 Nassau St.

The Port Folio, Vol. 1 (1813). "A Masonic Oration on the Death of Brother William S. Bush," New York, NY: Bradford & Innskeep.

Transcript, France, Affaires étrangères, Correspondence Politique, États-Unis, vol. 9, 1779 (July–August), folio 123/23vo, Manuscript Division, Library of Congress, Washington, DC.

Upton, Emory (1904). *The Military Policy of the United States*. Washington, DC: Government Printing Office.

Wilkinson, James (1816). *Memoirs of My Own Times*. Philadelphia, PA: Abraham Small.

Newspapers

Alexandria Gazette, Alexandria, VA (*AG*); *American and Commercial Daily Advertiser*, Baltimore, MD (*ACDA*); *American Citizen*, New York, NY (*AC*); *American Sentinel*, Philadelphia, PA (*AS*); *Boston Daily Advertiser*, Boston, MA (*BDA*); *Cahaba Gazette*, Cahaba, AL (*CG*); *Caledonian Mercury*, UK (*CM*); *Charleston Courier*, Charleston, SC (*CC*); *Charleston Mercury*, Charleston, SC (*ChM*); *City of Washington Gazette*, Washington, DC (*CWG*); *Daily Dispatch*, Richmond, VA (*DD*); *Daily Evening Transcript*, Boston, MA (*DET*); *Daily Globe*, San Francisco, CA (*DG1*); *Daily Globe*, Washington, DC (*DG2*); *Daily National Intelligencer*, Washington, DC (*DNI*); *Daily Republic*, Washington, DC (*DR*); *Evening Post*, New York, NY (*EP*); *Evening Star*, Washington, DC (*ES*); *Hartford Courant*, Hartford, CT (*HC*); *Intelligencer, and Weekly Advertiser*, Lancaster, PA (*IWA*); *Kentucky Gazette*, Lexington, KY (*KG*); *Lancaster Ledger*, Lancaster, PA (*LL*); *Maryland Gazette*, Annapolis, MD (*MG*); *National Intelligencer and Washington Advertiser*, Washington, DC (*NI & WA*); *Niles' Weekly Register*, Baltimore, MD (*NWR*); *Pennsylvania Gazette and Weekly Advertiser*, Philadelphia, PA (*PG & WA*); *Philadelphia Inquirer*, Philadelphia, PA (*PI*); *Plain Dealer*, Cleveland, OH (*PD*); *South-Carolina State Gazette and Timothy's Daily Advertiser*, Charleston, SC (*SCSG*); *The States*, Washington, DC (*TS*); *The Sun*, Baltimore, MD (*TSB*); *United States Gazette*, Philadelphia, PA (*USG*); *Virginia Argus*, Richmond, VA (*VA*); *War Journal*, Portsmouth, NH (*WJ*).

INDEX